HANDBRIDGE

A CENTURY OF CHANGE

PHOTO — LEN MORGAN

Len Morgan

and

Noel St John Williams

Published by and on behalf of

Handbridge Area History Group

Chairman: Howard Stevens

10 Berkley Drive

Handbridge

CHESTER CH4 7EL

Tel: 01244 679909

ISBN 0 9547483 0 1

British Library Cataloguing in Publication Data: a catalogue record of this book is available from the British Library.

Design and layout by Ian Birchenough

Reprinted with corrections December 2004

Front Cover: Old Dee Bridge, Chester, and Salmon Fishermen at work.
P R Wrightson and Derek Smith.

Frontispiece: The Gateway to Handbridge.
Len Morgan

Printed by:

Bemrose Shafron (Printers) Ltd

11 & 21 Chaser Court

Greyhound Park

CHESTER CH1 4QQ

Acknowledgements

The authors and Handbridge Area History Group would like to thank the following individuals, staff and organisations for their generous help and advice in the preparation of this book including those who have given their copyright permission to publish:-

His Grace, the Duke of Westminster; the Halifax Bank of Scotland plc; Marks and Spencer; Chester City Council; the staffs of Chester Community History and Heritage Centre, Cheshire and Chester Record Office, and of Cheshire Libraries, Information and Culture Service; Chester Chronicle; Chester Observer; Chester Courant; Imperial War Museum; Councillor Terry Ralph; Heads of all Handbridge schools; Principal of West Cheshire College; Richard Towndrow and the Queen's Park Residents Association and Adele Edwards and the Friends of the Meadows; Handbridge shopkeepers; Pat McGrath, ex-landlady of the Ship Inn; Canon Christopher Samuels of St Mary's and Rev Liz Blair of United Reformed Church; Terry Kelly; Gillian M G Brown; Eileen Simpson; Emma Stuart; Peter and Betty Winder; Derek Smith; Geoff Reynolds; Don Scarl; Mike Penny; Peter and Margaret Byatt; Father Francis Maple; Father Peter Sharrocks; Peter Bamford; Martin Meredith; Ruth Davidson; Howard Stevens; Ian Birchenough; Reg Barritt; Dilys Dowswell; John Gerrard; Jill Massey; John Tomlinson; Eliza Moore; David Baldwin ...

and all those who have kindly provided donations, photographs, materials and memories to make this book possible.

The authors have tried to identify and credit copyright holders and apologise for any omissions. In Section 7, most images are credited to the schools and college concerned.

Handbridge Area History Group – Founding Committee 20th December 2001

PHOTO — PHILIP MACEY

PHILIP MACEY		HOWARD STEVENS	GERALD PUGH
NOEL ST JOHN WILLIAMS	SARAH OSWALD (HERITAGE CENTRE)	ISOBEL FLEMING	LEN MORGAN

Major-General The Duke of Westminster K.G. O.B.E. T.D. D.L.

Portrait donated by The Duke of Westminster

Eaton Hall
Chester
CH4 9ET

My family has had a long and close association with Handbridge and its citizens. It is, therefore, with much pleasure that, as Patron of its local History Group, I write the Foreword to its first publication—

20th Century Handbridge

The contributions of my family to the amenities and social life of Handbridge are well documented in the book, and I am especially pleased that the Eaton archives have been used to add to the story. As I look through the pages, I note the depth of research that has gone into the book and the wealth of photographs and personal memories provided by the churches, pubs, shops, schools and individuals. Clearly, this is a project popular with and strongly supported by the local community.

This book is a fascinating account, well told in word and picture, of the events and changes in Handbridge's recent past. I commend it to all who enjoy a good story and wish the History Group every success in its initiative.

THE DUKE OF WESTMINSTER KG OBE TD DL

PHOTO — LEN MORGAN

Contents

Salmon to grace the
tables of Eaton Hall

Jill Kemp

vi

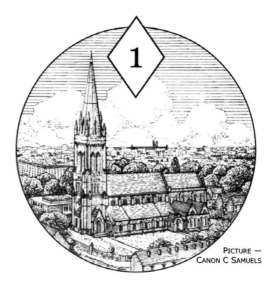

PICTURE —
CANON C SAMUELS

Roman Soldier to Queen Victoria

This book tells the story of Handbridge in the 20th century – mainly in pictures.

Earlier writers have given Handbridge scant respect. In 1882, for instance, George Ormerod described Handbridge as:

> *'A populous suburb of Chester consisting of narrow streets built on a red rock almost exclusively inhabited by the lower orders.'* (History of Cheshire)

Thomas Hughes was even less flattering:

> *'We might, if we chose, wander forth into Handbridge, were there anything in that suburb deserving of our special notice.'* (Stranger's Handbook to Chester—1856)

These were 19th century historians writing of an industrial age. We shall tell a very different story.

◆————————————————◆

The Romans and the River Dee

In AD 76, the Romans established the legionary fortress of Deva on a sandstone ridge in a loop of the River Dee. On the lowest practical crossing on the opposite bank, the settlement of Handbridge was born. Its sandstone quarries provided the stone to build the garrison and the city walls (depicted in stone in the Town Hall porch). A relief of the goddess Minerva, worshipped by the quarrymen, still survives, carved on the rockface in Edgar's Field. The Roman ford was replaced by a wooden bridge (*Handbridge = HĀN-BRUGGE – bridge on the rock/stone*). Handbridge became the southern exit from Chester to North Wales and to London via Roman Watling Street (modern Eaton Road).

PHOTO — IAN BIRCHENOUGH

ROMAN SOLDIERS BUILDING THE WALLS OF CHESTER.

PHOTO — LEN MORGAN

THE RELIEF OF MINERVA IN EDGAR'S FIELD

From Romans to Normans

Little is known about Handbridge after the departure of the Romans circa AD 410, who left Deva a deserted city. Its fortunes would have been linked with Chester, which became the capital of the Kingdom of Gwynedd for over 200 years. It was fought over and laid waste by Saxon, Northumbrian (607) and Danish (893) invaders. In 875 the bones of St Werburgh, the daughter of the first Christian King of Mercia, one of the Anglo Saxon kingdoms, were brought from Hanbury, Staffordshire, to Chester (eventually to be enshrined in the cathedral) for greater security against the invading Danes.

In 907 Ethelred, Earl of Mercia and his wife Ethelfleda, daughter of Alfred the Great, restored the city and its walls and Chester recovered some of its former glory.

In 973 shortly after his coronation at Bath, King Edgar held his court (in a place which is still called Edgar's Field) in Handbridge. He summoned to Chester eight of his Scottish/Celtic tributary kings *'to row him up the Dee to the church of St John and thence back to his palace'* (Higden's Chronicles) to show his overlordship of the whole of Britain.

The original can be seen in the Bull and Stirrup, George Street/Upper Northgate Street, Chester ▼

EDGAR the PACIFIC BEING ROWED DOWN THE RIVER DEE BY EIGHT TRIBUTARY PRINCES

PHOTO — MIKE PENNEY

Norman Handbridge

With the Norman Conquest, a new era began. In 1066, after the Battle of Hastings, William I came to the North crushing rebellion by force. c1077 he conferred the new title of Earl of Chester on his nephew, Hugh Lupus, granting him vast estates in Cheshire including Handbridge, which had formerly been held by the Saxon Earl of Mercia. Hugh Lupus built the first mill on the Dee and the causeway across it to drive the mill wheels. His Jolly Miller (who *'...cares for nobody and nobody cares for me ...'*) had the monopoly of grinding the corn for Chester, while Hugh retained the tithes for milling. In 1297 the Old Dee Bridge was built of stone on seven arches and fortified with towers, drawbridge and portcullis.

The original can be seen in the porch of Chester Town Hall ▼

HUGH LUPUS, CREATED EARL OF CHESTER.

PHOTO — IAN BIRCHENOUGH

Medieval Handbridge

During the 13th and 14th centuries Chester reached it zenith as a seaport, exporting raw and tanned hides, cloth, wool, pottery and grain, and importing wines, hops and bales of skins from Ireland for gloves and shoes. By the 15th century both its trade and importance as a port would decline with the silting up of the river. To protect Chester from Welsh attacks, in 1400, an outer gateway was built at Handbridge. So often was the suburb destroyed by fire, that it was called Treboeth (*burning town*) and today no medieval buildings remain in Handbridge.

Handbridge and the First Civil War (1644 – 46)

In the Civil War Chester declared for the King and suffered heavily in the two year siege; Handbridge was largely destroyed. The attacking Parliamentary force built its lines around Handbridge, following its contours, denoted by today's Eccleston Avenue, Beeston View, St John's Road and Queen's Park Crescent. The Overleigh Road to Mold and North Wales (along which Charles I escaped on horseback) was blocked by the Roundheads at Hough Green.

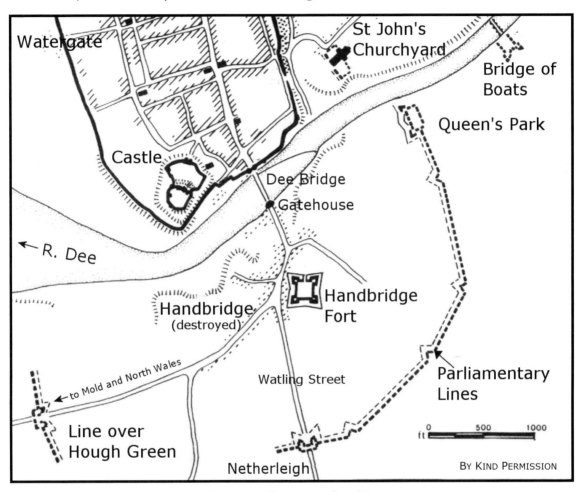

HANDBRIDGE DURING THE CIVIL WAR
Based on Grosvenor Museum Archaeological Report № 4 Civil War 1642–6. *S Ward 1987*

The Ancient Manor of Handbridge

The ancient manor of Legh, held by the Barons of Halton, was divided into Overleigh ('Upper Legh') and Netherleigh ('Lower Legh'). These, with the Royal manor of Handbridge, are mentioned in the Domesday survey of 1086.

Netherleigh was located at the Saltney end of the manor of Legh where, according to Hemingway (History of the County of Chester – 1831), it had a moated site. In 1735, the Stanleys of Alderley sold Netherleigh to a Chester draper, John Cotgreave, who owned strips of land in the medieval common field system in Handbridge and Claverton. His son, Thomas Cotgreave, built a new Netherleigh House c1780 in Eaton Road, transferring the name Netherleigh from Saltney to Handbridge. He wanted to take advantage of Eaton Road becoming fashionable at this time as the Grosvenors' approach to Eaton Hall. It was used as 'a boarding school for young gentlemen' in Victorian times under the Rev William Theophilus Giles MA, preparing boys for the Universities and Public Schools. (*Gazetteer of Chester* 1874)

In 1813, during the excavation of a cellar in the house, a considerable number of large cremation urns, lamps and a Roman sacerdotal figure were unearthed, guarded by a black stone lion. Some of these Roman discoveries can be seen in the Grosvenor Museum. Other cremation urns have been discovered along Eaton Road (Watling Street), demonstrating the Roman custom, regulated by law, that all burials should take place outside the fortress walls. Many of these burials were situated beside main roads, where passers-by could pay their respects.

PHOTO — LEN MORGAN

◄ NETHERLEIGH HOUSE, A GRADE II LISTED GEORGIAN BUILDING

In c1230 **Overleigh** manor was granted to the monks of Basingwerk Abbey, who built a chapel there. In 1545 Matthew Ellis, a gentleman of the bodyguard of Henry VIII, purchased the ancient timber manor house and estate of Overleigh from the Crown. During the siege of Chester (1645-6), the house was demolished but was later rebuilt by Thomas Cowper. Thomas was the son of the royalist mayor of Chester (1641-2), who had stood beside Charles I and Sir Thomas Gamul, watching from the city walls the defeat of the King's army at Rowton Moor in September 1645.

THOMAS HUGHES — MEMOIR OF REV W H MASSIE
JOURNAL OF CHESTER ARCHAEOLOGICAL SOCIETY 1857

◄ OVERLEIGH HALL
WILLIAM HENRY MASSIE, BORN AT No 3 STANLEY PLACE (1806), WAS A PUPIL AT THE HALL. HE BECAME RECTOR OF ST MARY'S-ON-THE-HILL.

On the north wall of St Mary-on-the-Hill, Chester, is inscribed on a wooden tablet:

Here lies Interr'd Mathew Ellis of Over-leigh in þe County of þe City of Chester; one of þe Body Guard to King Henry 8; Son of Ellis ap Dio ap Griffith Successor to Kenrick Sais A British Nobleman & lineally Descended from Tudor Trevor Earl of Hereford. He died 20 Apr. 1574; … His Son Mathew Ellis, of Over-Leigh, Gent. Died 1575, … Having issue Julian, who was married to Thomas Cowper of Chester Esqr …

Underneath, along with the Cowper coat of arms, are the words:

William Cowper, of Over-Legh, Esqr, … He died 12th October, 1767. Aged 66

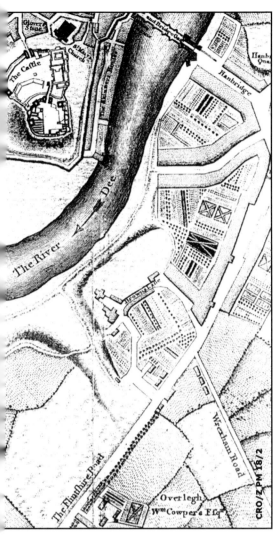

1745 MAP (PART) BY ALEXANDER DE LAVAUX
SHOWING OVERLEIGH HALL AT THE BOTTOM

The site and layout of the new Overleigh Hall are shown on Alexander de Lavaux's map of 1745, as being the site of today's new Overleigh Cemetery. The Hall remained in the Cowper family for nearly 400 years, before being demolished in 1838 by the Marquess of Westminster, in order to build a new approach to Eaton Park from Overleigh roundabout. The name Overleigh is still remembered in a school, a cemetery and the road in Handbridge.

Employment in Handbridge

Even before Roman times, **salmon fishing** was established on the Dee and became associated with Greenway Street (formerly Sty or Stig Lane). In the 11th century Hugh Lupus granted 60 fisheries above the weir to his dependants and tithes on all fish caught to the monks of St Werburgh's. Fishing provided the chief employment in Handbridge into the 19th century, catches being sent to the markets in Manchester and Liverpool. Important, too, for Handbridge's prosperity were its market gardens and extensive nurseries.

Greenway Street was a tight knit community, a breed of men now vanished from our society. Every salmon fishing season brought the familiar sights and sounds of fishermen laughing and joking together, as they mended and tarred their nets at the 'stakes' (rows of poles set six feet apart and used for hanging the nets). The boats were all made of wood, 16 – 18 feet long, shallow of draft and beamy, very estuarial vessels. Every Sunday morning, the Salvation Army came to play in the lane – half an hour of rousing music and hymns, accompanied by the ear-shattering beat of the big drum.

'Cheshire Within Living Memory'
Cheshire Federation of Wives' Clubs, 1994 p31

GREENWAY STREET C 1890S
INCLUDING MANY BUILDINGS LONG SINCE DEMOLISHED

NICHOLLS' TOBACCO AND SNUFF MILLS

Over the centuries other industries have flourished along both sides of the river: rope makers, skinners, tanners, paper makers, Hooley's candle factory and a needle factory. Handbridge housed the tobacco and snuff works of Thomas Nicholls & Co., established in 1780. These industries provided employment for many local people, both male and female.

John Swarbrick Rogers, merchant and glover, owned a prosperous skinning and tanning business near the Dee Bridge. In 1820, he built Greenbank (now the catering department of the West Cheshire College) and was mayor of Chester in 1821 – 2.

The Tithe Map of St Mary's parish (1842) indicates that Handbridge and Queen's Park were, for the most part, **pasture and arable land**, chiefly owned by the Marquess of Westminster and the Cotgreaves, rented out to small farmers. A comparison with the Ordnance Survey map of 1908 (i.e. 70 years later) shows little change to the farms, nursery gardens and allotments. Remembered today are Dickson's nurseries (site of Queen's Park School to Pinfold Lane), Fishwick Farm (Queen's Park), Stan Dutton's Queen's Park nurseries (St George's Crescent), Witter's Pinfold Farm (site of Pinfold Court), Johnson's Dairy (Brown's Lane), Powell's Farm (Old Wrexham Road) and McHattie's market garden (Grosvenor Nurseries – Overleigh Road/Old Wrexham Road). Above Greenway Street was Baker's Farm providing dairy products for the village.

The Victorian Era

One of the features of 19th century Chester was the considerable development of housing on the south bank of the Dee, which included the two wealthy residential areas of Curzon Park and Queen's Park. The latter was a villa estate laid out in the middle of the century by Enoch Gerrard with some of the houses designed by James Harrison. In guide books, Queen's Park was praised for its commanding position and beautiful river scenery.

The latter half of the 19th century would see many changes in local government, education and health, which would affect Handbridge and the lives of its citizens. In 1888, Cheshire County Council was established and Chester was given county borough status. Local health boards were created to provide better housing and sanitation. Board schools were created in 1870 for elementary education to the age of 13, with compulsory education to the age of 10 in 1880.

Like many industrial areas in Victorian England, Handbridge had its share of poor housing and insanitary conditions. Workers were crowded into 'courts' off the main roads between Mill Street (Harrison's, Jones' and Coach Courts), Greenway Street (Jones', Edgar and Copperas Courts) and Overleigh Road (Bannister's, Brook's, Wooley's etc.). These unhealthy 'courts' would be condemned and demolished in 1928 to be replaced by half-timbered shops and better quality housing around 1930.

During the century the churches were the leading providers of education, especially for the poor. Before 1870, the Church of England established a training college for teachers in Cheyney Road (1839) (the first outside London) and day schools, including Handbridge Infant School (1828—60). The Wesleyan Methodists opened a day school in St John's Street (1839—1909) and the Catholics St Werburgh's Schools in Queen Street (1854), St Francis' in Cuppin Street (1883) and a boarding school, Dee House Ursuline Convent School (1854).

The Grosvenor Legacy

Handbridge has benefited much over the years from the generosity of the Grosvenor family. Hugh Lupus, for example, the 1st Duke of Westminster, presented Edgar's Field with its Roman shrine to the City in 1892. In 1887 he had built and donated to the community, the Church of St Mary-without-the-Walls (following re-organisation of parish boundaries), the school and rectory followed, in 1895, by the Men's Institute.

HUGH LUPUS 1ST DUKE OF WESTMINSTER (1825—99) ▶

PRINT OF AN 1872 PORTRAIT BY SIR JOHN EVERETT MILLAIS
COURTESY OF CANON CHRISTOPHER SAMUELS
(ORIGINAL IN THE POSSESSION OF THE GROSVENOR FAMILY)

A TOKEN OF APPRECIATION BY HANDBRIDGE CITIZENS!
THE ARCH WAS ERECTED AT THE JUNCTION OF OVERLEIGH AND EATON ROADS. THE BUILDING IN THE CENTRE IS ON THE SITE OF THE MEN'S INSTITUTE. IT WAS THE 'OLD HOUSE AT HOME' PUB, ALSO KNOWN AS THE MAYPOLE. IN 1850, THE LICENSEE WAS SAMUEL CROSBIE. THE COTTAGES ON THE RIGHT HAD BEEN DEMOLISHED BY 1886 TO MAKE WAY FOR ST MARY'S CHURCH AND SCHOOL. ▼

DUKE OF WESTMINSTER—PP 13/227

Long live the NOBLE PAIR, Under GOD'S Paternal CARE.

May the FOUNTAIN of LOVE for ever supply, Streams flowing with blessings from Heaven on high, On the EARL and his BRIDE united this day. Come friends keep the Wedding shout, hip! hip! huzza!

May their hearts with love abound, To the needy all around.

BY KIND PERMISSION OF THE DUKE OF WESTMINSTER

The Century Ends

At the end of the 19th century, Britain stood at the height of her imperial and economic power, with Queen Victoria firmly established in the nation's affections and ruling over a quarter of the world's population. The last of her colonial wars, the Boer War (1899—1902), is commemorated in Handbridge by Pretoria (5th June 1900) Terrace, and Mafeking (17th May 1900) Terrace opposite—now the postal address for both is Pretoria Street.

PRETORIA STREET TODAY WITH THE ORIGINAL PRETORIA TERRACE 1900 SIGN CARVED IN STONE
PRETORIA TERRACE IS ON THE LEFT OF THE STREET, MAFEKING TERRACE ON THE RIGHT (SIGN NO LONGER VISIBLE)

In 1901 Queen Victoria died. As a young lady, she had formally opened the Grosvenor Bridge in 1832 and passed through Handbridge on her way to stay at Eaton Hall. With her death, the Victorian age was over. The 20th century had begun.

PRINCESS VICTORIA, AFTER OPENING AND NAMING THE GROSVENOR BRIDGE ON 17TH OCTOBER 1832, 'PASSED OVER THE OLD BRIDGE, WHERE SHE WAS CHEERED BY MEMBERS OF THE ROYAL YACHT CLUB AND BOAT CREWS ON THE RIVER, AND THEN THROUGH HANDBRIDGE (A HUMBLE NEIGHBOURHOOD) TO EATON HALL'.

(ROYAL VISITS AND PROGRESSES P. 458)

The River Dee
& Salmon Fishing

A RARE SIGHT ON THE DEE—A FISHING BOAT WITH A SAIL

PHOTO—JOHN GERRARD

The River Dee

Rising as a bubbling spring in the Welsh Mountains above Lake Bala, the River Dee, celebrated in verse and song, flows down via Corwen, Llangollen and Holt to Chester and thence to the open sea by way of Saltney and the Dee estuary.

Many wooden bridges were built until in 1297 a bridge was finally constructed in stone. Our stone bridge with its seven irregular arches dates back to 1382. The bridge was widened in 1826 to include a footpath. Tolls were abolished on 1st January 1885 and traffic lights installed 1937/38.

THE RIVER AT LOW WATER CLEARLY SHOWS THE SITE OF THE ROMAN FORD ▼

PHOTO—LEN MORGAN

AN EDWARDIAN SCENE ON THE OTHER SIDE OF THE BRIDGE ▼

COURTESY OF PHILYS DOWSWELL — POST CARD 1908

Chester. The Groves. Evening.

THE OLD DEE MILLS C1900
ACROSS THE RIVER FROM HANDBRIDGE CAN BE
SEEN FROM LEFT TO RIGHT:
PART OF THE CASTLE BUILDINGS, THE MASSIVE
BUILDINGS OF THE DEE FLOUR MILL, ST
MARY'S-ON-THE-HILL, AND THE FORMER
COTTAGES TO THE RIGHT OF THE BRIDGEGATE.

▲

THIS EARLY 20TH CENTURY PHOTOGRAPH,
LOOKING TOWARDS HANDBRIDGE, SHOWS THE
FLOUR MILL (LEFT), THE RIVERSIDE COTTAGES
AND THE SHIP INN ON THE FAR SHORE. THE
FLOUR MILL WAS FINALLY DEMOLISHED IN
1910 AND REPLACED IN 1913 BY THE HYDRO
ELECTRIC GENERATING STATION. ▶

FROM THE SAME POINT OF VIEW AS THE TOP PHOTOGRAPH ABOVE, ALMOST A CENTURY LATER, FROM LEFT TO RIGHT:
COUNTY HALL (OPENED IN 1957 ON THE SITE OF THE COUNTY GAOL), ST MARY'S-ON-THE-HILL, AND, TO THE RIGHT OF THE BRIDGEGATE, THE
NEW FLATS AND EDGAR HOUSE. THE WEIR ENABLED WATER TO BE CHANNELLED TO THE MILLS.

The tidal bore is a high wave of water that rushes up the river at times of exceptionally high tides (e.g. Spring) and enters a long, narrowing estuary. The height of the bore is greater near the banks than at midstream.

PHOTO—LEN MORGAN

NOTE HOW THE BOAT HAS BEEN LIFTED BY THE BORE.

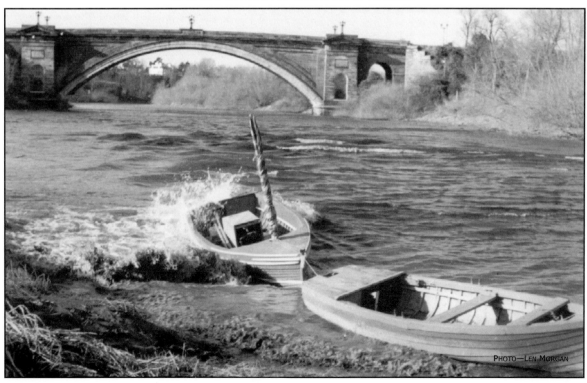

PHOTO—LEN MORGAN

AT THE START OF THE CENTURY THE VIEW UP THE RIVER FROM THE WEIR INCLUDED THE 'FLOATING' BATHS (LEFT), THE FIRST
SUSPENSION BRIDGE AND THE OLD MILLS ON THE HANDBRIDGE SIDE.
BY 1903 THE BATHS HAD GONE AND THE MILLS HAD BEEN REPLACED BY THE PREMISES OF THOMAS NICHOLLS & SON
(SEE BELOW)

PHOTO—COURTESY OF STEPHEN LANGTREE

THOMAS NICHOLLS & SON HEAD OFFICE AND FACTORY WITH WESTERN COMMAND IN THE BACKGROUND

PHOTO—LEN MORGAN

SALMON LEAP FLATS ERECTED ON THE SITE OF THE FACTORIES IN THE 1960S (SEE PAGE 6)

THE FLOUR MILL WAS FINALLY DEMOLISHED IN 1910 AND REPLACED IN 1913 BY THE HYDRO ELECTRIC GENERATING STATION, SEEN BELOW UNDER CONSTRUCTION IN 1912 AND AS IT WAS IN 2001.

PHOTO—P WRIGHTSON

The site of the Flour Mill

Here in the 1600s, eleven water wheels were at work—six for grinding corn, two for pumping water and three for fulling mills to clean and treat cloth.

PHOTO—LEN MORGAN

◄ MILLWHEEL PADDLE AND MILL RACE NEXT TO THE OLD TOBACCO FACTORY, SALMON LEAP

PETER AND SUSAN MORGAN STANDING BY THE ORIGINAL WATER-WHEEL OF THE SNUFF MILL—1963 ▼

PHOTO—CHESTER CHRONICLE

PHOTO—LEN MORGAN

The Grosvenor Bridge, designed by Thomas Harrison (1744—1829), soars 'like a rainbow across the River Dee'. It was, at the time, the largest single span stone arch in the world (200 feet). The bridge was opened by Princess Victoria in 1832. Harrison, a carpenter's son, born in Richmond (North Yorkshire), was not only a remarkable architect but a great engineer. His best known work was the Castle complex (1788—1822). He died in 1829, aged 85, leaving William Cole and Jesse Hartley to complete the Bridge. Thomas Telford, John Rennie and Isambard Kingdom Brunel, three of Britain's leading engineers, were consultants in the project

Nowhere can be seen through the arch of the bridge.

PHOTO—LEN MORGAN

▲ NOWHERE WAS ORIGINALLY TWO SMALL COTTAGES, Nᵒˢ 1 & 2, NOWHERE. IT WAS CONVERTED INTO ITS PRESENT, SINGLE HOUSE BY A MR LEWIS c1960

PHOTO—P WRIGHTSON

THE GROSVENOR BRIDGE'S NEW STREET LIGHTING WAS INSTALLED IN 1930, THE SAME YEAR THAT CHESTER TRAMS FINISHED RUNNING. IN THIS PHOTOGRAPH, THE METAL POLES SUPPORTING THE ELECTRIC CABLES HAVE BEEN REMOVED BUT THE TRAM LINES REMAINED. THEY WERE LATER SURFACED OVER WITH TARMAC.

AN AERIAL PHOTOGRAPH OF THE RIVER DEE TAKEN C1960

BOTTOM LEFT IS THE RACE COURSE, THE ROODEE WITH THE GRACEFUL ARCH OF THE GROSVENOR BRIDGE NEXT TO IT. THE OLD CEMETERY CAN JUST BE SEEN IN THE WOODED AREA, BOTTOM RIGHT. IN THE CENTRE OF THE PHOTOGRAPH IS THE OLD DEE BRIDGE WITH THE WEIR JUST UPSTREAM. TO THEIR LEFT ARE THE CASTLE COMPLEX, ST MARY'S-ON-THE-HILL AND COUNTY HALL. ON THE OPPOSITE SIDE OF THE RIVER STANDS ST MARY'S WITHOUT-THE-WALLS AND JUST ABOVE, THE BUILDINGS WHICH ARE NOW QUEEN'S PARK HIGH SCHOOL. QUEEN'S PARK WITH ITS SUSPENSION BRIDGE, THE MEADOWS AND THE SOUTHWARD CURVE OF THE DEE OCCUPY THE TOP RIGHT PORTION OF THE PICTURE

SUNDAY AFTERNOON ON THE RIVER
THE RIVER DEE—A SOURCE OF PLEASURE
A POSTCARD FROM 1910 LOOKING TOWARDS THE OLD DEE BRIDGE AND SHOWING THE FIRST SUSPENSION BRIDGE

POST CARD—R GREEN P.O, SALTNEY
COURTESY OF DILYS DOWSWELL

St. Marys Without-the-Walls Church and Rectory Chester. 1903

PHOTO—WILL BUCKLEY

WILLIE GERRARD AND HENRY SCONCE FISHING FOR SALMON IN THE EARLY 1950S

◄ A POST CARD TO MISS MABEL CROSS, C/O THE REV STONE, THE VICARAGE, NEW BRIGHTON – 'WITH VERY BEST WISHES AND HOPING YOUR COLD IS BETTER. LOVE FROM CONNIE'

Salmon fishing was probably established on the Handbridge bank of the River Dee long before the Romans. For many generations Handbridge has been the home of a close knit community of mainly fishermen's families centred on Sty Lane, now called Greenway Street.

▼ THE FUNERAL OF JOHN BELLIS OF 54 GREENWAY STREET, 1ST SEPTEMBER 1926 (SEE PP 20, 22 & 153)
HIS COFFIN IS SURROUNDED BY A LARGE CROWD OF FRIENDS, NEIGHBOURS AND MEMBERS OF THE SALVATION ARMY

PHOTO—COURTESY OF THE LATE FRED WARREN, FOUNDER (1941) AND FOR MANY YEARS, THE POPULAR MUSICAL DIRECTOR OF THE CESTRIAN MALE VOICE CHOIR

▲ Hauling the nets back into the boat after completing a draught—1960s

▲ Eagerly waiting to see what has been caught in the 'Purse' in the centre of the net—1930s

▲ After being caught, the fish had to be sold!

▲ Each end of the net is drawn in by a fisherman to enclose the central 'Purse' 1930s

Photo—Elizabeth Hughes

◀

Salmon fishermen moored opposite Greenway Street retrieving the net after having completed a draught—early 1900s. Rowing the right hand boat is John Dobson, whose son is pulling in the net with Edward Bingley. The boy rowing the left hand boat is Billy Woodworth.

PHOTO—MAY ROSEDALE (DAUGHTER OF ELIJAH BUCKLEY)

◄ NED BUCKLEY WITH HIS SON EDWARD AND BROTHER TOM WITH THEIR RECORD CATCH OF 40 SALMON (MARCH 1948). THE CATCH WAS BOUGHT FOR THE PRINCELY SUM OF £148 13S 4D BY FISHMONGERS T L WILKINSON & SON OF THE CROSS, CHESTER (SEE OPPOSITE PAGE)

The Salmon Netting Season

The 1937 River Dee salmon netting season opened at midnight on Tuesday, 14th March, with the usual keen competition among Handbridge fishermen to catch the first fish and thus qualify for the Guinea First Prize offered by the Rector of St Mary's, the Reverend A W Sarson*. The first fish was taken in a boat owned by Mrs H Woodworth of Greenway Street by Arthur Smith aged 16 of Nowhere, River Lane, and Wilfred Maguire. It was a 15 pounder, retailed in Chester at 3/6d per pound.

The record holder for the biggest catch of the season was Mr John Spencer, who caught 29 fish on 23rd March 1937 weighing a total of 405 lbs.

*The Rector's prize, started in 1882, was originally a ton of coal for the first salmon caught in the season. Later rectors awarded one guinea.

PHOTO—MAY ROSEDALE (DAUGHTER OF ELIJAH BUCKLEY)

◄ ELIJAH BUCKLEY AND BROTHER JOHN WITH A 36 LB SALMON CAUGHT IN 1948

NOT ONLY SALMON WERE CAUGHT IN THE DEE! A 4 FOOT LONG PORPOISE, WEIGHING 1½ CWT, WAS NETTED ▼ BY R BUCKLEY & SON ON 22ND AUGUST 1932

Best Catch for 40 Years

Mr John Randles of St Martin's Fields with brother Mr Peter Randles in a boat owned by Mrs Sarah Jones (see p. 22) of Greenway Street was fishing at 11am last Thursday on lower Draught, close to the Cop. 'We felt something heavy in the net but did not dream we had caught such a beauty—42½ lbs. It took the two of us all the time to lift the salmon into the boat,' John said. The salmon was sold to Messrs Wilkinson, The Cross, and attracted a lot of attention.

Chester Observer, 30th March 1940

PHOTO—WILL BUCKLEY

FISHERMEN IN THE 1950s ▲

L TO R: ARTHUR ROSEDALE, JOHN BUCKLEY, THOMAS BUCKLEY, ELIJAH BUCKLEY, JACK BUCKLEY
BEHIND: SNIPE JOHNSON (IN THE TRILBY)

Joseph and Mary Anne Buckley, the parents of Arthur Rosedale's wife, May (not shown), were born and bred in Greenway Street. They had 17 children (of whom 8 sons and 2 daughters survived). Joseph went blind and Mary Anne brought up her family alone in their two bedroom house in Greenway Street. They received a letter of thanks from King George V for their five sons serving their country in France during World War I. All five returned to join their three brothers in fishing their father's boats between them as a family business.

As well as the Buckleys, Johnsons and Rosedales (above), other well-known fisher families were the Gerrards, Prices, Randles, Spencers, Tottys, Bellises and Whites—passing on the age old tradition from father to son.

▼ PART OF A FISHING (DRAFT NET) LICENCE DATED 12TH MAY 1908 FOR JOHN CAMPBELL OF 2, PARADISE, HANDBRIDGE. THE LICENCE WAS DUE TO EXPIRE ON 31ST AUGUST 1908. IT AUTHORISED JACOB MAYNARD AND SAMUEL MAYNARD TO WORK AT ONE TIME.

▲ MIKE JOHNSON, SALMON FISHERMAN AT NOWHERE

SALMON AND FRESHWATER FISHERIES ACTS 1861 TO 1892.

A No. 46

DEE FISHERY DISTRICT.

LICENSE TO FISH FOR SALMON IN PUBLIC OR COMMON WATERS WITH MOVEABLE INSTRUMENTS.

WE, THE BOARD OF CONSERVATORS, appointed for the Fishery District of the River Dee as defined by a Certificate of the Board of Trade, dated the 8th day of November, 1890, deposited in the Office of the Clerk of the County Council of Denbigh, do by virtue of the powers vested in us under the Salmon and Freshwater Fisheries Acts 1861 to 1892, hereby license *John Campbell* of *2 Paradise Handbridge Chester* in the County of *Chester* to fish with one **DRAFT NET** for Salmon in any waters within the said District in which there is a Public or Common right of fishing for Salmon.

This License will expire on the Thirty-first day of August, 1908.

GIVEN under the Seal of the said Board, this *12th* day of *May* 1908.

Signed *J. Edward* Distributor

DRAFT NET LICENSE — £5 — 200 yards.

THE STAKES

THE SALMON NETS WERE DRIED BY STRETCHING THEM OVER WOODEN POLES STAKED IN THE GROUND. SOME EVENTUALLY TOOK ROOT AND FORMED THE TREES THAT CAN BE SEEN TODAY!

◄ VIEW OF STAKES c1950

PHOTO—LEN MORGAN

THE STAKES FROM A DIFFERENT PERSPECTIVE VIEW FROM RIVER LANE c1970 ▼

PHOTO—LEN MORGAN

A GROUP OF SALMON FISHERMEN PREPARING THE BOATS AND NETS FOR A DAY'S FISHING—FEBRUARY 1960
NOTE—NOWHERE, NEAR TOP LEFT AND HARRISON'S MASTERPIECE, THE GROSVENOR BRIDGE, TOP RIGHT

A GROUP (MAINLY FISHERMEN) AT THE ENTRANCE TO EDGAR'S FIELD BESIDE THE SHIP INN

◄

LEFT TO RIGHT:
JACK CAMPBELL, "INA" JONES, TOMMY BELLIS, JOHN GERRARD (CHESHIRE REGIMENT, WOUNDED AT ANZIO, 1942), HARRY MILLARD

▼ SARAH JONES NÉE GERRARD, (EVAN TOTTY'S GRANDMOTHER) WHO DIED AGED 87, THE DOYENNE OF THE FISHING COMMUNITY OF GREENWAY STREET
PAINTING FROM A PHOTOGRAPH BY LEIGHTON WALMSLEY (1988)

SALMON FISHING STILL SURVIVES
PADDY RANDLES FEB. 1997

◄ THOSE OTHER DEE FISHERS—THE SWANS SHOULD NOT BE FORGOTTEN!
THESE BEAUTIFUL CREATURES GRACE THE RIVER WHETHER FEEDING OR, AS HERE, NESTING, EVEN AMIDST THE RIVER DETRITUS

Postscript:

The final journey taken by so many fishermen was a tribute paid by them to the river—the passage of the hearse over the two bridges, The Old Dee and the Grosvenor—a final salute of mutual respect. (See page 32)

Pubs and Shops

PHOTO—BOB JONES

MRS DAVIES'S SHOP—5 BRADFORD STREET, 1952/3

THE CHILDREN ARE COUSINS AND MRS DAVIES'S GRANDCHILDREN
ARTHUR DAVIES, DAVID JONES WITH BROTHER BOBBY AND COUSIN BARBARA DAVIES
OUTSIDE THEIR GRANDMOTHER'S SHOP
THE SHOP BECAME A GENTS' HAIRDRESSERS, A BOOKMAKERS AND THEN A PRIVATE HOUSE.

The Pubs

The 'Pub' is a national institution, a part of our history and traditions. Chester's wine-drinking Romans had their *tabernæ* (taverns), the Danes, Vikings and Saxons had their alehouses. For centuries, women brewed the ale, chiefly for home consumption. When beer ousted ale as the popular drink (c1500), the 'public' house was born and the inn provided accommodation.

Public houses adopted signs, often of local interest. Handbridge had its animals, monarchs, local gentry, and national heroes and events. (Note the names below).

19th Century Handbridge boasted many inns, taverns and public houses: The Coach and Horses; The Duke of Wellington; The Feathers; The Handbridge Tavern; The Hare and Hounds; The King's Arms; The Old House at Home; The Waterloo Inn; The Wheatsheaf. Today, only The Ship Inn, The Grosvenor Arms, The White Horse, The Red Lion and The Carlton (built in the 1920s) remain.

Young Women Not Wanted

Chester's taverns and ale houses had a dubious reputation in Tudor times and in 1540, the City promulgated the following order:—

'Whereas all the taverns and ale houses of this City be used to be kept by young women causing divers slanderous reports etc …To eschew such wantoness (sic), brawls, frays and other inconveniences … it is ordered that after the 9th of June next, no tavern or ale house be kept in the said City by any woman between 14 and 40 years of age, under pain of 40 pounds forfeiture for him or her that keepeth any such servant.'

Hugh Denson, Tales of Chester 1979

STAGE COACHES, OFTEN CARRYING MAIL, REGULARLY LEFT CHESTER FOR WREXHAM AND THE SOUTH. THEY WOULD HAVE CROSSED THE OLD DEE BRIDGE. ▶

The Ship Inn

IN AN IDEAL LOCATION FOR SERVING THE SHIPPING AND MILLING ACTIVITIES AROUND THE OLD DEE BRIDGE, A SHIP INN HAS BEEN SITED HERE FOR AT LEAST TWO CENTURIES

FROM AN ORIGINAL PHOTOGRAPH IN THE SHIP INN—IAN BIRCHENOUGH

▲ MINE HOST, PAT McGRATH, LANDLADY OF 'THE SHIP', BEHIND A WELL STOCKED BAR

PHOTO—JOHN GERRARD

▲ REG GRAY AND JOHN GERRARD AT THE SHIP 1947
THE GRAY FAMILY WERE LANDLORDS FOR OVER 50 YEARS

The Ship

The Ship is first mentioned in the directory of Chester in 1771 but the building is a lot older and is mentioned under that name in 1748 when the landlord was a Mr Walley. However, one record dating back to 1441 recalls 'ale hous' near or on the same site where a brawl took place over a lady of doubtful reputation. The men involved were fined 1s 6d each for disturbing the peace and the "lady" was confined in a house of correction for 7 days.

The name 'Ship' has connections with pilgrimages but in Chester the name 'Ship' and 'Sheep' are often confused. As the Old Dee Bridge was one of the major routes for sheep being brought to market, it is possible that the original name was 'The Sheep Inn'.

In 1784 John Bannister was fined for selling short measures.

In 1846 a James Morris was fined £2 2s 6d for poaching salmon and selling it in 'The Ship'. This was probably not an isolated instance as the pub was long popular with fishermen, both legal and illegal.

Between 1846-1849 William Dutton ran the pub but he also ran a wheelwright's from the same building, probably at the back.

In 1856 a rather gruesome murder was committed near the pub when William Jackson killed two young children and buried them in the garden nearby. A man leaving the pub saw Jackson leading the little boy away, although 'The Ship' was not mentioned by name. The execution was public and held in Chester Castle.

The street numbering in Handbridge has been erratic. In 1882, the address was given as No 6; today, it is no 18.

Licensees

1771	John Bannister	1840	James Duff	1915	R Gray
1792	Mrs Bannister	1846	William Dutton	1946	A Gray
1812	Thomas Griffiths	1869	Alexander Richardson	1983	N Wakefield
1834	James Clare	1882	Horne Simpson	1994	A Tatler
1828	Mary Davies	1907	R Higginson	1997	A Phelps

Extract from a document on the wall of The Ship Inn

Grosvenor Arms

Landlords of the Grosvenor Arms from 1855 to c1890 were Joinsons, an old Handbridge family, the origin of the name of today's Joinsons Court, adjoining the inn. The inn was run by the Clubbe family for over 40 years with Mrs Emily Clubbe (1910) being a long serving Landlord.

▲ SUN INSURANCE FIRE MARK PREVIOUSLY ON THE GROSVENOR ARMS. THE POLICY NUMBER IS SHOWN: 77J073

PHOTO—LEN MORGAN

▲ THE GROSVENOR ARMS (BETTER KNOWN BY LOCALS AS 'CLUBBIE'S')

Waterloo Inn

In 1840 the landlord was Joseph Greenway (the origin of Greenway Street?). Declared redundant c1922, the premises were occupied by H Stant (baker), L King (clothes), Pearl Antiques, Felicity's Ladies Hats and today is Nueva Vida (Spanish Properties).

PHOTO—LEN MORGAN

Duke of Wellington

NO 31, THE DUKE OF WELLINGTON INN WAS ► DEMOLISHED IN 1928/9 TO MAKE WAY FOR THE NEW SHOPS. THE INN OCCUPIED THE SITE OF H K CROSSLAND (GROCER) AND TODAY'S MARTIN'S NEWSAGENTS AT 31 HANDBRIDGE. FOR THE LAST TWENTY YEARS OF THE INN'S EXISTENCE THE LICENSEE WAS WILLIAM HANMER.

PHOTO—LEN MORGAN

THE DUKE OF WELLINGTON FISHING CLUB PICTURED OUTSIDE THE PUB C1900 ▼

PHOTO—JOHN TOMLINSON

The 1881 census shows nine soldiers in billet at The Duke of Wellington Public House (and 20 more in private houses in Handbridge). They were members of the 1st Royal Cheshire Militia.

Like today's Territorials, they were part-time soldiers (5 years) undergoing twenty one day's annual training at The Militia Barracks, demolished in 1959 to be replaced by Cheshire Police Headquarters

White Horse Inn

There were frequent changes of landlord of the White Horse Inn, until the Simmonds family took control c1906—1930.

Its address varied from 60 to 64 and 68 Handbridge.

THE WHITE HORSE INN IN THE EARLY PART OF THE 20TH CENTURY. PARADED OUTSIDE ARE THE JAVELIN MEN WHO ESCORTED THE JUDGE TO THE ASSIZES AT CHESTER CASTLE

Hare and Hounds / King's Arms

The Hare and Hounds was remarkable for its variations of address—149, 117 Handbridge, Old Wrexham Road and 81 Overleigh Road.

Its last landlord was John Hanmer, brother of the landlord of The Duke of Wellington.

The King's Arms' was administered by the Speed family for the last 30 years of its existence. It was declared redundant c1922.

OLD WREXHAM ROAD AT THE JUNCTION WITH OVERLEIGH ROAD.
THE FIRST HOUSE ON THE CORNER WAS THE HARE AND HOUNDS AND THE SECOND HOUSE WAS THE KING'S ARMS. BOTH PUBS CLOSED IN 1922 AND ARE NOW PRIVATE HOUSES.
PICTURE TAKEN IN 1950.

PHOTO—MRS YORK NÉE SPEED

About 1902 Licensing Magistrates were empowered to close premises which they regarded as redundant and the local Committee proposed to take action with the two adjoining premises in Old Wrexham Road. To save her pub from closure, the licensee of The King's Arms engaged a Birkenhead solicitor who had won similar cases. A successful plea enabled the pub to remain open for another 20 years when, again, it was declared redundant. The landlady was asked why the decision to close the house this time had not been contested. She replied that she was unable to engage her former advocate—hardly surprising since the Birkenhead solicitor was now Lord Birkenhead, the Lord Chancellor.

A Handbridge Miscellany 1964

The Red Lion—first licensed in 1781

The Red Lion was rebuilt in 1904. In 1912 its landlady was Mrs Emily Maria Humphreys (c1875—1917) who died aged 71. The licence then passed to her daughter, Miss Emily Humphreys, affectionately known as 'Miss Em'. She died on 3rd October 1971, aged 93. Her younger brother, Harry, died of wounds in France, 1915, aged 30. Miss Em's spirit is said to haunt the pub, still remembering the time when a pint of beer cost 3½d and whisky, 2d.

PHOTO—FROM A POST CARD

THE RED LION IN 1912 UNDER LANDLADY, MRS EMILY MARIA HUMPHREYS
THE WIDE DOORWAY TO THE RIGHT OF THE PUB LED TO THE 'ROPEWALK', THE FACTORY OF JOHN HARKER, ROPE AND BRUSH MAKER. THE COTTAGES (FAR RIGHT) HAVE BEEN REPLACED BY OVERLEIGH MEWS

COURTESY OF MARTIN MEREDITH
THE CHRONICLE 3 SEP 1971

CHESTER'S OLDEST LICENSEE, MISS EMILY HUMPHREYS, AGED 93 OF THE RED LION INN, PULLING PINTS FOR THE PAST 54 YEARS.

The Carlton Tavern

PHOTO—LEN MORGAN

In 1905/06 No 1 Hartington Street was occupied by the Carlton Hotel (Mary Tomkinson) and No 3 by E Powell (grocer). The Carlton Tavern replaced three cottages (nos 1, 3 and 5) which were demolished to make way for the new tavern in the 1920s. Hence, the next house to the Carlton Tavern is No 7.

A HOPEFUL BAND OF FOOTBALL ▶ SUPPORTERS OUTSIDE THE CARLTON TAVERN BEFORE THEIR AWAY TRIP TO SEE CHESTER PLAY AN FA CUP 4TH ROUND REPLAY AGAINST STOKE CITY IN JANUARY 1947
AN OPPORTUNITY TO SEE STANLEY MATTHEWS IN HIS HEY-DAY WAS TOO GOOD TO MISS! CHESTER LOST THE REPLAY 3-2 AFTER DRAWING 0-0 AT SEALAND ROAD.
MICKEY MORAN (CENTRE) WAS THE TEAM MASCOT. TOP LEFT IS JIMMY WALSH, A FORMER CHAMPION BOXER. THE LANDLORD IS SHOWN FRONT FIRST RIGHT WITH HIS SON BEHIND HIM.

Handbridge Shops

The early century poverty-stricken courts and tenements in Handbridge were replaced by good sanitation and attractive housing. However, the major change can be seen in its public houses and shops. Once Handbridge boasted three butchers, three greengrocers, two chemists, two dairies (Johnsons and Uptons), one bank and Mealings, the ironmongers (subsequently replaced by The Jolly Miller Café, which itself has been replaced by an antiques shop).

PHOTO—FROM A POST CARD

HANDBRIDGE, CHESTER.

▲ LOOKING DOWN HANDBRIDGE MAIN STREET TOWARDS THE OLD DEE BRIDGE
REBUILT IN 1928—1930 IN THE DISTINCTIVE BLACK AND WHITE ARCHITECTURE. NOTE THE POLICE BOX BEHIND THE TREE ON THE RIGHT.

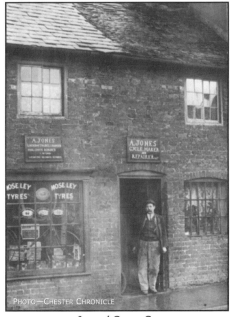

PHOTO—CHESTER CHRONICLE

▲ JONES' CYCLE SHOP
WAS SITUATED TOWARDS THE OLD DEE BRIDGE END OF THE ROW OF SHOPS IN HANDBRIDGE c1920 BUT WAS LATER TO OCCUPY 2 MILL STREET

PHOTO—LEN MORGAN

▲ LINDA OF BOUSTEAD BLAND ANTIQUES, NO 2 MILL STREET
THE SHOP HAS SEEN A NUMBER OF OCCUPANTS INCLUDING W H MEALING AND THE JOLLY MILLER CAFE

EXTRACT FROM PHILLIPSON & GOLDER'S DIRECTORY 1900–01

HANDBRIDGE, EAST
(FROM OLD DEE BRIDGE).

(MILL STREET)

Nicholls, T. & Co., tobacco and snuff manufacturers
Jones and Sons, tobacco and snuff manufacturers
7 Hughes, W. J., shopkeeper
13 Oswell, H. E., baker
15 Ellis, C., hairdresser
17 Webb, H., Coach and Horses inn
23 Oswell, H. E., Wheatsheaf inn
25 Snelson, G., shopkeeper
27 Stout, M., fishmonger
29 Hillier, T. (greengrocer)
31 Jones, J., Duke of Wellington inn

(QUEEN'S PARK ROAD)

33 Jones, T
35 Bridgewater, John, Congregational Chapel
37 Willcock, J.
39 Graham, Thomas, bootmaker
41 Edwards, T.
43 Crossley, J.
45 Rigby, J.
47 Speed, T

(BELGRAVE PLACE)

55 Croft, S.
57 Gregg, Thomas
59 Birch, J.
65 Newstead, R. (Witcombe Villa)
67 Hilton, R., St Mary's cottage

(EATON ROAD)

St Mary's (Handbridge) Young Men's Friendly Society and Men's club

OVERLEIGH ROAD.

COTGREAVE TERRACE

71 Orme, J.
73 Mulvey, Miss, grocer & provision dealer and post office
75
77 Mulvey, E. M., joiner
79 Edwards, J.
81 Marchant, S. R.
83 Sheldon, S.
85 Gerrard, R. G.
87 Hindley, Mrs.
89 Dutton, T.
91 Williams, R.
93 Pritchard, J. E.
97 Hickey, J., butcher
105 Humphreys, Mrs. E. M., Red Lion inn
Harker, J. and Co., rope and twine manufacturers
McHattie & Co., seed merchants and nurserymen
139 Sconce, Ellen, shopkeeper
141 Williams, Mrs., nurse
143 Nabb, Miss A. L.
145 Edwards, Thomas, cowkeeper

OLD WREXHAM ROAD

Griffiths, Mr., Hare and Hounds
Speed, Mrs., King's Arms
Powell, T., market gardener and cowkeeper
McHattie, Miss

EXTRACT FROM KELLY'S DIRECTORY 1975

HANDBRIDGE

Continuation of Lower Bridge st to 1 Eaton rd
East side
.............here is Mill st.............
1 Higgins J. T. drug store
3a Shepherd Arth
3 Vogue Hairdressing, ladies' hairdrssrs
5 Chick O'Dee, grocer
5a Richardson Edwd
7 Upton F. G. newsagt., (CH4 7JE). Tel. Chester 22174
7a Barry Rt
9 Elizabeth, draper
9a Whitley M. E.
11a Cook Jn
11 Walker & Cain, fruitrs
13 Cheetham A. & Son, boot mkrs
13 Cheetham Albt
15 Visitatela, gift shop
15 Beedleston H. E.
17a Cobden Wltr
19 Bateman W. confctnr & post office
19a Bateman Wm
.....here is Queen's Park rd .....
Handbridge Service Station
Handbridge Congregational Church
33 Houghton Arnold
39 Gibson Thos
41 Edwards Florence
43 Allman Geo
45 Johnson Jn
...... here is Connahs court.......
47 McGuigan Jas
49 Giles Dorothy
51 Probert Thos. J
.... here is Belgrave pl..........
53 Tilston M. J
55 Mulvey, E. M., joiner
57 Dickinson Geo
59 Taylor Cyril
61 Thomas Fredk.W
.... here is Ebury pl............
65 Duffell Michl R
67 White Gordon
.... here is Eaton rd............

West side
Bridge Cottages

2 Harvey Miss S
4 Randles J
6 Dobson Wm
8 Harvey S. J
10 Spencer B. C.
12 Williams Leonard

St John's View

2 Hull Albt
4 Davies Fredk. Wm

18 Ship Inn
Edgar Field Recreation Ground
20 King L. & Co. (Chester) Ltd departmental store
22 Lowndes & Coward, fried fish dlrs
24/26 Weinholt Carl, baker
28 Baynes Mrs. A. M
......here is Joinson's court ......
30 Brown J. greengro
32 Grosvenor Arms PH
42 Hanmer Arth
44 Dunne Patrick J
44 Murphy B. A
........here is Edgar court.........
48 Wilson Alfreda
50 Gentile Saml J
52 Wild H. greengro
.... here is Greenway st........
54a Parker Edwin
54/56 Edge E. W. & Son, butchers. Tel No 20931
58a Walkersons (Insurance Brokers) Ltd, insur brkrs
58 Hockenhull & Co, business transfer consultants, valuers & estate agents. Tel. Chester 26914 & 26621
62 Davies Rt
64 Wiseman Mrs. Martha J
66 White Horse P.H
68 Poole Regnld
70 Weaver Fredk. Thos
72 Bebbington Geo
........here is Overleigh rd ....

OLD WREXHAM RD.

From 81 Overleigh road
West side
2a Hanmer Wm
2 York Geo. F
4 Ince Geoffrey
6 Smith Michl
8 Davies Maurice H
East side
1 Randles Patrick
St Bede's Secondary School (Roman Catholic)
Overleigh Secondary School

▲ 'DADDY' HUGHES OUTSIDE HIS GREENGROCER'S SHOP BESIDE HARRISON'S COURT IN 1918

▲ NO 15 IS NOW A FLOWER SHOP, THE 'SECRET GARDEN' NO 17, IS NOW 'HANDBRIDGE INTERIORS' ▼

▲ MIKE REYNOLDS OF 'GEORGES, THE BIG MAN'S SHOP' NO 13 HANDBRIDGE
ESTABLISHED IN 1986, THE SHOP AND INTERNET COMPANY SELLS OUTSIZE MEN'S CLOTHES AND FOOTWEAR AND IS RUN BY MIKE AND ROSEMARY, AND THEIR SON, DAVID. NO 13 WAS, IN 1964, CHEETHAM'S SHOE REPAIRERS. ▼

THE POST OFFICE WAS ORIGINALLY AT 11 OVERLEIGH ROAD; IN 1930, IT MOVED INTO NEW PREMISES AT 11 HANDBRIDGE AND THEN INTO ITS PRESENT LOCATION, Nº 19 ▼

THE POST BOX HAS THE 'GR' ROYAL CYPHER WITH NO NUMBER INDICATING THAT IT IS FROM THE REIGN OF KING GEORGE V (DIED 1936) ▼

Wild's Greengrocers

▲ Mrs Dorothy Wild and Judith outside the Shop No 52 Handbridge

▲ Herbert Wild and his son, Michael, in Eaton Avenue c1960. Herbert's cart was a well known sight around Handbridge and the nearby areas long after the days of the horse drawn carriage had gone.

▲ Samantha Wild, Herbert's granddaughter helping out her dad during school holidays August 1988

▲ Herbie Wild's horse and cart outside the original shop, No 52 Handbridge in 1964 Later, the business moved to No 58, next door to Edge's—bottom left picture

Herbert Wild's funeral, 28th October 2003
The hearse and his cart passed over the two bridges as tradition demanded

Ernest W Edge & Son

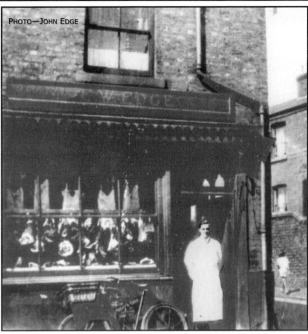

ERNEST EDGE (FATHER OF JOHN) SHORTLY AFTER OPENING HIS BUSINESS IN 1937 (ABOVE AND BELOW)
THE TOP PHOTOGRAPH WAS USED AS A MODEL FOR THE TILE-WORK AT THE BACK OF THE REFURBISHED SHOP

FLORRIE WITH JOHN EDGE IN 1941 ▲

◄ SON, JOHN EDGE, LAUNCHING THE REFURBISHED SHOP INTO THE NEW MILLENIUM—DECEMBER 2001

Weinholts of Chester

Frank Weinholt opened the bakery and shop in 1953 with his wife Irene and sister Margaret. His son, John, joined the firm in 1974 and opened another shop at the Bache, Upton (1976). A larger shop followed in 1984 in Watergate Street, managed by daughter Ann. With daughters Karen and Jane joining the family business, Weinholts are now a by-word for quality baking and confectionery, including special cakes for Royal occasions. The shop in Watergate Street has since closed but a shop in the former Woolpack Inn, Northgate Street Row, opened in 1992.

PHOTO—MRS MOORE

PHOTO—LEN MORGAN

▲ MRS ELIZABETH (ELIZA) MOORE WHO WORKED AT WEINHOLTS BAKERY FOR 50 YEARS

◄ THE *CELEBRATION CAKE STUDIO* WAS FORMERLY LOWNDES CHIP SHOP

▼ FORMER COTTAGE NOW KERR'S INSURANCE NEXT TO THE GROSVENOR ARMS
NOTE THE ORIGINAL FIREPLACE (L)

PHOTO—LEN MORGAN

PHOTO—LEN MORGAN

▲ NEXT DOOR TO WEINHOLTS IS THE ENTRANCE TO THE FORMER JOINSON'S COURT, WHOSE COTTAGES ARE NOW ALL DEMOLISHED

▲ CELEBRATING THE 50TH ANNIVERSARY OF VE DAY IN THE VICINITY OF JOINSON'S COURT, MAY 1995 JOAN WALKER (L) AND ETHEL HORLEY (R)

▲ 'HANDBRIDGE INTERIORS' (NO 17) SELLING SOFT FURNISHINGS.

JUDITH CRILLY OF 'THE SECRET GARDEN' (NO 15) A FLOWER SHOP ▶

PHOTO—PETER WINDER

THE GROSVENOR STORES, QUEEN'S PARK VIEW, HANDBRIDGE (EST 1923) ▲

QUEEN'S PARK VIEW

IN 1929, THREE SHOPS WERE BUILT ON WASTE GROUND LOCALLY KNOWN AS 'THE BANK' :—

MRS S A ORMES (No 15, CONFECTIONER AND TOBACCONIST; NOW QUEEN'S PARK STORES)

EDWARD'S CHEMISTS (NO 14 WAS W ADAMS DOTCHIN; NOW CRUMBS)

C WINDER (NO 13 WINES AND PROVISIONS— THE GROSVENOR STORES; NOW THE DRINKS CABIN, AN OFF-LICENCE)

◄ IN THE DOORWAY ...
LEFT: A SHOP ASSISTANT
CENTRE: WINNIE EDWARDS
RIGHT: ANNIE WINDER (PETER'S MOTHER)
WITH BICYCLE: THE ERRAND BOY
(SEE PAGE 112) THE CHURCH WHIT PARADE MARCHED OVER THIS PLOT OF LAND BEFORE THE SHOPS WERE BUILT

PHOTO—LEN MORGAN

PHOTO—LEN MORGAN

FROM TOP LEFT, CLOCKWISE:

- THE DRINKS CABIN OFF-LICENCE IN THE SAME PREMISES AS WINDERS'.

- ANNA RIDEAL (L) AND RUTH CLARK (R) OF THE DRINKS CABIN.

- 'CRUMBS' IN THE SAME PREMISES AS EDWARD'S CHEMISTS

- ANN MARIE TREACY (L) AND MARY OLIVER (R) OF CRUMBS

- SISTERS JULIE AND LYN IN HANDBRIDGE GENERAL STORE, THE SAME PREMISES AS ORMES

Photographic Goods
L. Edwards M.P.S.
Medical & Surgical Requirements
14 QUEEN'S PARK VIEW,
HANDBRIDGE, CHESTER
TELEPHONE 25025

PHOTO—LEN MORGAN

PHOTO—LEN MORGAN

PHOTO—LEN MORGAN

The War Years

PHOTO—LEN MORGAN

THE CROSS OF SACRIFICE
NEW CEMETERY, HANDBRIDGE
DESIGNED BY SIR REGINALD BLOMFIELD

4th August 1914—Britain Declares War on Germany

Handbridge Men Volunteer to Join the Colours

There was almost a continuous stream of men presenting themselves at Chester Castle in all sorts of garb, a man in a tail coat and straw hat standing shoulder to shoulder with a labourer in begrimed corduroys and red neck scarf.

Chester Observer, Established 1852

BY THE KING

A PROCLAMATION

FOR CALLING OUT THE ARMY RESERVE (INCLUDING THE MILITIA) AND EMBODYING THE TERRITORIAL ARMY

GOD SAVE THE KING

PICTURE CREDIT—IMPERIAL WAR MUSEUM Q48378A

4000 Men Under Canvas in Handbridge

From a field off Rake Lane, 2000 men and 1000 horses left camp and marched down Eaton Road and through Chester to Northgate Station, where they embarked for France in thirteen special trains. Men from Belgrave Place, Hartington Street, Eaton Road, Pyecroft Street, Overleigh Road, Greenway Street and The Mount, Queen's Park were among them, serving with the Cheshire Yeomanry. Crowds lined the streets cheering and bidding Farewell!

Not since the Roman days have the streets of Chester resounded as continuously to the troops of trampling horses and the tramp of armed men.

Chester Observer, 22nd August & 5th September 1914

Mayor of Chester tries to stop 'panic buying'. 'Business as Usual' in shop windows. Appeals for parcels for the Forces.

Lord Kitchener asked for 100,000 men. By Christmas, 1 million had joined up.

Volunteers drilled in parks, squares and schoolyards in civilian clothes, carrying dummy rifles.

PHOTO—COURTESY OF LEN MORGAN

▲ OFFICERS OF 1ST BN, THE CHESHIRE REGIMENT PRIOR TO GOING TO FRANCE, 1914

After bidding a tearful 'farewell' to their menfolk, women began to face the problems of running a family, of increasing food shortages and rationing. Trades Unions resisted women taking over men's jobs and for the first two years women were considered suitable only for clerical jobs. Soon, however, married women teachers were recruited (normally women teachers 'retired' on marriage). From 1915 crèches were introduced. In Cheshire, 2000 women were trained and placed on farms. By 1916 the Government called for women to volunteer to replace men in factories, shops, offices and on buses and the railways. These changes would lead to a social revolution in dress, habits and independence—trousers, short skirts, bobbed hair, the use of cosmetics, smoking in public and, for women over 30, the vote!

Chester Ladies' Silver Thimble Fund

This organisation raised money for a motor ambulance car. It was handed to the Mayor at a Garden Party given by Mr and Mrs E Peter Jones at their 'At Home', Greenbank, in aid of the Belgian Relief Fund.

1916

Silent Film Shows at the Men's Institute

I can remember enjoying the weekly silent films at the Men's Institute shown in the evenings with 30 to 50 people attending during the Great War. Performance times were advertised in the shop window of 45 Handbridge owned by Mrs Alice Leigh beside the Red Lion Public House.

Memories of my Grandmother
Mrs Julia Hunt (née Wilcox)

Mr and Mrs W H Mills of 11 Belgrave Place, Handbridge, received a special mention of Proud Families serving King and Country with 3 sons and 4 nephews in the Armed Forces. Their eldest son, William Arthur, is in the Royal Field Artillery; Thomas Henry is in the 5th Cheshire Regiment (TA) and Charles Leopold is on HMS Eclipse in the North Sea. Mr Mill's father was a C/Sgt at Chester Castle, his eldest brother is a Quarter Master Sgt and another brother went through the South African War.

Chester Chronicle—26th September 1914

▲ 5TH BN CHESHIRE REGT (TA) AT A CAMP IN ABERYSTWYTH BEFORE GOING TO FRANCE AND FLANDERS IN 1915

Four Handbridge soldiers were killed on active service with this battalion – George Bird, James Hubert, Leslie Dutton and Samuel Maynard.

Soldiers Who Died in WW I, 1989

Food Rationing

1917 Growing scarcity of food, especially milk and eggs: 'No Beer' notices in pubs

1918 (March)—Ration Cards were issued for meat and butter and margarine.

Five Sons in the Army

Handbridge has well answered the call for King and Country. We heartily congratulate Mrs Astbury, Harker's Rope Walk, who has five sons serving in the Army. We think this is a record for Handbridge.

Albert is in the Royal Field Artillery, Alfred, George and William in the 5th Cheshire Territorials and Andrew in the RAMC.

Courant, 10th March 1915

To: Mrs Astbury, Harker's Rope Walk, Handbridge
From: Privy Purse Office, Buckingham Palace.
12th March 1915

Madam,

I have the honour to inform you that the King has heard with much interest, that you have, at the moment, five sons in the Army. I am commanded to express to you the King's congratulations and to assure you that His Majesty much appreciates the spirit of patriotism, which prompted this example in one family, of loyalty and devotion to their Sovereign and Empire.

Your Obedient Servant

F M Ponsonby
Keeper of the Privy Purse

Chester Chronicle

A feature of World War I was the appalling loss of life in the armed services with the mounting casualty lists appearing in the newspapers amongst other more cheerful news.

Heroes Come Home

This week a train load of wounded soldiers arrived 'direct from the trenches' for dispersal among local hospitals. Many women sobbed openly as the wounded passed through Chester to their destinations including Eaton Hall, which the Duke of Westminster has offered as a hospital for wounded soldiers and sailors. He had volunteered for active service with the Cheshire Yeomanry.

Chester Observer, 9th January 1915

THE COMMONWEALTH WAR GRAVES COMMISSION MAINTAINS 2410 WAR CEMETERIES. HEADSTONES ARE OF A STANDARD PATTERN, SHOWING NO DISTINCTION OF MILITARY OR CIVIL RANK, RACE OR CREED. INSCRIPTIONS SHOW SERVICE OR REGIMENTAL BADGES WITH A SIMPLE MESSAGE, SUCH AS 'THEIR NAME LIVETH FOREVERMORE', CHOSEN BY RUDYARD KIPLING, WHO LOST HIS SON IN THIS WAR. 'KNOWN ONLY TO GOD' IS CHOSEN, WHERE THE INTERRED HAS NOT BEEN IDENTIFIED.

PHOTO—LEN MORGAN

▲ ROLL OF HONOUR, ST MARY'S CHURCH HANDBRIDGE HAS NO PUBLIC WAR MEMORIAL BUT THERE ARE ROLLS OF HONOUR IN ITS TWO CHURCHES AND IN QUEEN'S PARK HIGH SCHOOL.

PHOTO—LEN MORGAN

HANDBRIDGE CEMETERY

RICHARD JONES OF CONNAH'S COURT, HOME ON LEAVE, 1915 ▶
SHOWN HERE WITH HIS WIFE, ETHEL AND DAUGHTERS MABLE AND DAISY;
RICHARD WORKED ON THE EATON ESTATE.

FAMILY PHOTOGRAPH

◀ LETTER SENT TO MRS HARRIET BIRCHENOUGH (IAN'S GRANDMOTHER) ON THE DEATH OF HER SON, 24922 BOY WALTER KEENE OF THE CHESHIRE REGIMENT, ON 7TH JULY 1918

Royal Sympathy

The King commands me to assure you of the true sympathy of His Majesty and the Queen in your sorrow.

He, whose loss you mourn, died in the noblest of causes.

His country will be ever grateful to him for the sacrifice he has made for Freedom and Justice.

Signed

Secretary of State for War

<table>
<tr>
<td>

A HAPPY CHRISTMAS and GOOD LUCK TO OUR NAVY and ARMY

Chester Observer, 1915

</td>
<td>

<u>Chester Newspapers appeal for good causes:</u>

Wounded War Horses; Starving Belgians; Hospitalised Casualties; The Mayor's Fund for the Red Cross; books for Cheshires in the trenches.

25th May, Empire Day—special street collections for Lord Robert's Memorial Workshops for Disabled Soldiers

</td>
</tr>
</table>

War Dead: Notifications of war dead continued to increase especially after 1st July 1916, the Battle of the Somme. Some of Handbridge's dead are buried in Overleigh Cemetery: many of the dead have no known graves.

▼THIEPVAL MEMORIAL

BATTLE OF THE SOMME
1ST JULY—18TH NOVEMBER 1916
THERE ARE 600 BRITISH AND FRENCH GRAVES. THE NAMES OF 72,000 BRITISH SOLDIERS WITH NO KNOWN GRAVE ARE INSCRIBED ON THIEPVAL MEMORIAL, DESIGNED BY SIR EDWIN LUTYENS AND MAINTAINED BY THE COMMONWEALTH WAR GRAVES COMMISSION. EACH YEAR A MAJOR CEREMONY IS HELD THERE ON 1ST JULY.

PHOTO—NOEL ST JOHN WILLIAMS

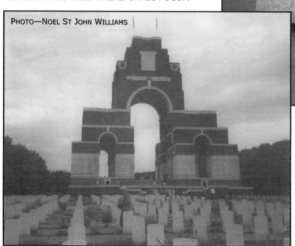

PHOTO—NOEL ST JOHN WILLIAMS

RIFL. J BLACK 1084 (21) ▲

12 BN. ROYAL IRISH RIFLES, KILLED THIEPVAL, 1ST JULY 1916. UNCLE OF MRS CHRISTINA ST JOHN WILLIAMS.

2ND LT. RUPERT R NEWSTEAD (28),

17TH BN. THE KING'S LIVERPOOL REGIMENT (ATTACHED TO 13TH BN. CHESHIRE REGIMENT), DIED 7TH JULY 1916. SON OF PROFESSOR ROBERT AND ELIZABETH NEWSTEAD, 67 HANDBRIDGE.

CHRISTINA, WIFE OF CO-AUTHOR, NOEL ST JOHN WILLIAMS, LOST THREE UNCLES IN WORLD WAR I. NOEL'S FATHER, A CAPTAIN IN THE 1ST BN CAMBRIDGESHIRE REGT, WAS WOUNDED IN FRANCE, 1916

"At the going down of the sun, and in the morning, we will remember them."

Armistice Day—11th November 1918

16th Nov 1918	Mayor announces Armistice from the Town hall steps
18th Dec 1918	Special entertainment at the Royalty Theatre to raise funds for local War Hospitals and Christmas gifts for the wounded.
30th Jan 1919	300 re-patriated soldiers entertained at the Town Hall.
25th Apr 1919	1st Bn. Cheshire Regiment returns to enthusiastic welcome. Prayers held for 'Fallen Comrades'.
3rd May 1919	End of Food Rationing by coupons.
28th Jun 1919	Peace Treaty signed between Allied Powers and Germany.
11th Jul 1919	Peace Day Celebrations. Street tea parties and sports etc in schools.
27th Aug 1919	3300 'returned heroes' in Victory Parade in Chester. Handbridge streets are full of cheering crowds and festooned with bunting and flags.

World War II (1939—1945)

Handbridge Prepares

1st July 1939: Cheshire County Council ordered the testing of blackout arrangements in offices, shops and domestic premises, and street lighting. Chester was declared ' not a vulnerable area' for civil defence purposes but 'a reception area for refugees' under the Government Evacuation scheme. Petrol rationing was introduced and the public asked to shop early, so that shops could close before dark.

Air Raid Precautions announced for Handbridge 23rd September 1939	
Warden Posts	Congregational Church: 27, Eccleston Avenue: 21, Eaton Road: 76, Handbridge: 1, Devonshire Place: 22 & 133 Appleyards Lane: Tentry Heys, Queen's Park.
Air Raid Siren	Water Tower
First Aid Depot & Reception Centre	Men's Institute
Auxiliary Fire Service	Moore and Brock

Every Household should have a First Aid Box and prepare a shelter.

G Burkinshaw, Chester Town Clerk

Photo—Len Morgan

Photo—Ron Reynolds (Father is in the centre row 4th left)

▲ Auxiliary Fire Service (AFS) based at Moore and Brock (site of residential home behind the Petrol Station) Replaced by AFS Station in Queen's Park (No 16 St John's Road)

Photo—Len Morgan

▲ AFS Station, Queen's Park (sign still visible) Opposite St John's Road

Air Raid ► Precaution Badge worn by various ARP Services including Air Raid Wardens

◄ Machine Gun Bunker in the fields at the side of Eaton Road. It is still visible

WILLS'S CIGARETTES

ARP

AIR RAID PRECAUTIONS BADGE

1940 – Winston Churchill becomes Prime Minister 10th May

10th May: The War begins in earnest when the Germans invade The Netherlands and Belgium.

13th May: Churchill's famous 'Blood and Toil' speech to the nation.

4th June: Dunkirk falls after The British Expeditionary Force is evacuated.

10th July: The Battle of Britain—Three month air war ending on 30th October.

'Never in the field of human conflict has so much been owed by so many to so few.'

Boats from the River Dee that went to Dunkirk
Raglan—returned intact: **Ronnie**—damaged, repaired and returned: **Nelson**—Sunk by a mine.

PHOTO—CHESTER CHRONICLE

The first list of Army casualties is announced. Eaton Hall becomes a Convalescent Home for Service patients. The Women's Voluntary Service (WVS) appeals for books, magazines etc. for the wounded and the Cheshire Regiment.

◀ THE HOME GUARD MARCH PAST CHESTER TOWN HALL

23rd July: Local Defence Volunteers becomes the Home Guard (Dad's Army). War work was done during the day, training and duty at night and weekends. Handbridge men join 'A' Company, 71 Cheshire HG under Major H T Hedley, whose wife ran the shop opposite St Mary's Church. HG – Women Auxiliaries enrolled in 1943.

22nd June: Public Air Raid Shelter is built for 150 people in Edgar's Park. The Public may use schools' surface shelters and trenches during the holidays. Schools are to remain open.

28th Nov: A landmine explodes over Handbridge

PHOTO—PETER WINDER

▲ PETER WINDER (LEFT) OF 11 ECCLESTON AVENUE, JOINED THE EAST LANCASHIRE REGIMENT IN 1940. HE TRANSFERRED TO THE ROYAL SIGNALS FOR SERVICE IN INDIA AND BURMA.

Sgt James Jones, whose mother and sisters live in Meadows Place, Handbridge, has been serving with the Royal Marines for 16 years and is currently attached to HMS Exeter. He took part in the Battle of the River Plate (13th Dec 1939), which resulted in the defeat of the German Battleship, Graf Spee.

Chester Chronicle 20th January 1940

PHOTO—MRS PAM BUTLER

▲ SAM (HOME ON LEAVE FROM RAF) AND PAM BUTLER, 24 BEESTON VIEW

The Home Front

From 1939 to 1940 women volunteers worked in Civil Defence, Women's Land Army, munition factories and non-combatant roles in the Armed Services. By 1941 conscription of women (those between 14 and 64 were registered) had been introduced. By 1944 almost all women, married and single, were employed either full or part-time in factories, workshops and/or at home.

Many Handbridge housewives joined the Women's Voluntary Service, working from home. Duties included supplying cups of tea to workers and casualties, looking after the elderly and providing shelter for the homeless. They were trained in First Aid and fire-watch duties. Some wore uniforms, some armbands.

WOMEN'S LAND ARMY APPEALS FOR VOLUNTEERS 'OF GOOD PHYSIQUE, ▶
AGED BETWEEN 18 AND 35'.
COURANT 1ST JANUARY 1941
(*PICTURE CREDIT—IMPERIAL WAR MUSEUM LDP 324*)
AUDREY BANHAM (NÉE NELSON) OF 34, ECCLESTON AVE AND BETTY ELLAM OF
EATON AVE WERE TWO WHO VOLUNTEERED.

Morrison 'table' shelters are being made available free for Householders without any form of air raid shelter, domestic, communal or public, whose income does not exceed £350 per annum. An exhibition has been arranged in Handbridge Congregational Church 12th—17th January 1942 from 9am—9pm daily. Courant

▲ HEADSTONE ON THE GRAVE OF FIREMAN C G DUTTON
AND THE SCROLL COMMEMORATING HIS DEATH WHICH IS HUNG IN
CHESTER FIRE STATION ▶

This scroll commemorates
Fireman C.G. Dutton
Chester Fire Brigade
held in honour as one who served King and Country in the world war of 1939-1945 and gave his life to save mankind from tyranny. May his sacrifice help to bring the peace and freedom for which he died.

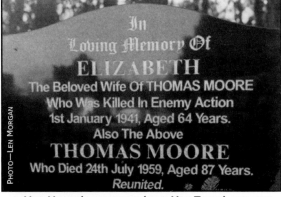

▲ MRS MOORE'S DAUGHTER (NOW MRS TOTTY) AND TWO
GRANDCHILDREN SURVIVED THE RAID WHICH KILLED
ELIZABETH MOORE FROM HANDBRIDGE.
ALL WERE RELATED TO THE TOTTY SALMON FISHING FAMILY RESIDING
IN OVERLEIGH ROAD.

A Schoolgirl's View of the War

The early days of the War were, for us, dismal, depressing and dark (because of the 'Black-out' Regulations). Some of our prefects left to join the Services. What will become of us? At night, the air raid sirens often disturbed our sleep. In the daytime, I remember filing out of school in a calm and orderly fashion to the air raid shelters situated across the road in front of the school. Dinners were served in the 'dug-outs'. When lessons were interrupted, we passed the time 'deep down' by singing songs and telling stories.

Rowena Delamere, The City High School for Girls (1940—47)
CRO/Z/DES/37

Footnote:

The air raid shelters ran parallel with the road with separate entrances at each end for boys and girls—and divided in the centre to make any hope of fraternisation impossible.

Joan de Winton (née Reynolds)

Handbridge Congregational Church housed a Warden's Post. During a raid on Liverpool , shrapnel (from a mobile AA gun operating on the outskirts of Chester) could be heard falling on the chapel roof. Two wardens failed to return from patrolling the area. When, eventually, they did return, they said that they had not been worried by the shrapnel: they had been sheltering behind a thick privet hedge!

R R Zanker
Handbridge Miscellany

The USA entered the war on 8th December 1941 after the Japanese bombed Pearl Harbour.

PHOTO—COURTESY BETTY WINDER

◄ GIS SORTING MAIL IN THE GPO
PAULINE FARLEY, A HANDBRIDGE GIRL WHO WORKED IN THE GPO, MARRIED JAKE GREENSPAN (4TH LEFT) AND BECAME ONE OF THE 70 000 UK GIRLS WHO MARRIED GIS IN THE WAR.

GIS SIGHTSEEING PRIOR TO D-DAY ►
PROFESSOR NEWSTEAD CONDUCTED A NUMBER OF 'LEARNING ABOUT BRITAIN' TOURS AROUND THE CITY WALLS FOR ALLIED TROOPS.

PHOTO—COURTESY BETTY WINDER

Betty Winder *of 2 Devonshire Place and 9 Eccleston Avenue was 18 when the war started.*

She remembers her friends joining factories and such organisations as GPO, WLA, WVS and also that GIs made good dance partners. She had to be home by 10:30 pm!

Grahame Jones *of Queen's Park, who was a schoolboy in 1943, remembers that the American servicemen quickly made an impact on the local community, handing out apples, oranges and bananas to local children and giving a friendly smile to everyone.*

My Wartime Memories

There was a unit of the American Army on Eaton Road with a large gated entrance opposite Appleyards Lane. It was a 'bell-tented' camp, which we used to call wigwams. German internees were held there: they were allowed out to do household chores: we had one at our house (132 Allington Place), who would clean out the coal fire, blacklead the range and wash the linoleum flooring.

The American soldiers practised building pontoon bridges across the River Dee between Pott's Rock and Eccleston Ferry (roughly in the area of the recent Heronbridge Roman excavations). We kids would ride on the metal sections as they were being installed and request 'Any gum, chum?'

During German bombing raids (usually on Liverpool), we would go to the air raid shelters when the siren sounded. They were underground in the field behind what is now the Salmon Leap apartments. They were dark and smelly and we walked on duckboards because the shelters were six inches under water. I remember bombs being jettisoned along Eaton Road and the iron railings round the Plantation opposite my house being removed for the war effort.

Don Scarl

Do it NOW!

CHESHIRE COUNTY SALVAGE DRIVE

May 30-June 13

KITCHEN WASTE

RUBBER

PAPER

METAL

RAGS

BONES

PICTURE—CHESTER CHRONICLE

Collect all your salvage *now*.
Get it ready in clean dry heaps
for your Council to collect — or
take it to the local dump.

Women at War
'The Nation, including women, must be mobilised to fight a total war.'

1941 **Mar** Call for 100 000 women to enter factories.

Dec All single women (20—30) were called up.

1943 **May** Women aged 18—45 liable for compulsory part-time war work. Loudspeaker vans tour Chester area to recruit women for vital jobs.

Engineering and Aircraft work; Railways; Ammunition inspection and packing; Industrial Canteens; Hospitals; Clothing manufacturing; Laundries; Shops and Offices; Fire Service (£2 15s 0d per week); Women's Land Army.

Diary of Rationing

1940 **Jan** Ham; Bacon (4oz); Sugar (12oz)

Mar Meat;

Jul Tea (2oz p.w.); Butter (4oz)

1941 **Mar** Jam; Marmalade; Syrup; Cereals

May Cheese (1oz p.w.)

June Clothes rationing introduced

Dec Points system introduced on tinned fruit, fish, vegetables, milk, rice etc.

1947 Bread and potatoes rationed

1954 Rationing of food ended.

Children received extra eggs, orange juice, cod liver oil and dried milk.

Newspaper Headlines

'Dig for Victory' **'Every potato and cabbage counts'** **'Make do and Mend'**
Salvage Collections for paper, rags metal, pig food, clothing etc. **Furniture rationed**
'Enterprise and Ingenuity' (eg Food Recipes) **Painted stocking seams.**
Queuing 'a way of life'.

Schools—1943

17th March Mr R F Challacombe, Head of Boys Grammar School, gives his first annual report: 'With so many fathers away on military service and mothers on war work, family life tends to falter. Schools can help with children's welfare.'

10th July Old Girls at City High School Reunion 'Old' girls relate their experiences at War: Mobile VAD; WLA; Services; Munitions; War-time Day Nurseries; Fire Services.

To Mothers

Please don't forget she plays her part.
Her feet are wet, her hands are cold.
The queues are long, the goods all sold.
No canteen, no unrationed meal
Reward her labours. Yet no squeal.

Crosville Buses
Chester Chronicle
20th February 1943

Wartime Celebrities Visit Chester and Western Command

ENSA (Entertainments National Service Association) concerts for units and hospitals starred many wartime celebrities e.g. Vera Lynn (We'll Meet Again); Gracie Fields; Tommy Trinder.

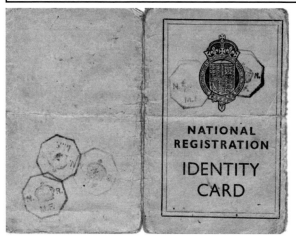

▲ NATIONAL IDENTITY CARD—FRONT AND BACK
THE CARDS WERE ISSUED IN SEPTEMBER 1939
'TO BE CARRIED AT ALL TIMES'

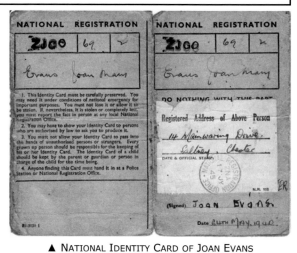

▲ NATIONAL IDENTITY CARD OF JOAN EVANS
(NOW JOAN MORGAN)—INSIDE PAGES
THIS CARD WAS ORIGINALLY ISSUED 24TH MAY 1940 BUT A CHANGE
OF ADDRESS SUPPLEMENT HAS BEEN ADDED.

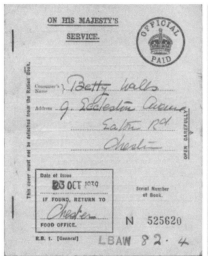

▲ THE RATION BOOK OF BETTY WALLS
(NOW BETTY WINDER)—FRONT

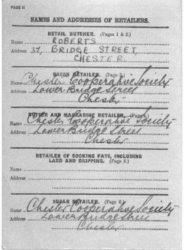

▲ RATION BOOK—INSIDE PAGE
SHOWING REGISTERED RETAILERS

▲ MOTOR FUEL RATION BOOK
COVER (TOP) AND INSIDE

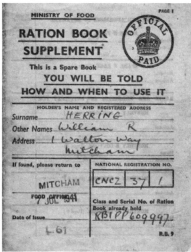

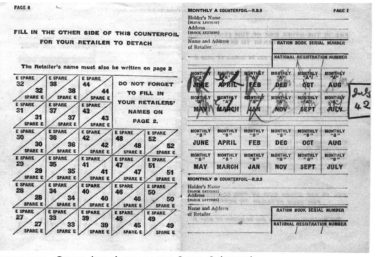

▲ RATION BOOK SUPPLEMENT—COVER (LEFT) AND PAGES 8 AND 9 (RIGHT)

Every member of the family had a ration book: adults (cream): children (green).

PHOTO—CHESTER CHRONICLE

▲ REFUGEES FROM LIVERPOOL ARRIVE AT CHESTER STATION

Handbridge Rest Centre

Rest Centres: Their purpose is to provide a temporary home for a few days, until other arrangements can be made.

After the Air Raid
What to do and where to go:

If enemy action has damaged your home so that you cannot live in it, or you have been told by the Police or Wardens to leave for the time being, by reason of the presence of unexploded bombs and you cannot go at once to relatives or friends, you should go to one of the prepared Rest Centres at which meals and temporary shelter are provided. The Wardens or Police will tell you to which of the Centres you should go.

Signed G. Burkinshaw,
Chester Town Clerk

200 Evacuees from London arrive at
Handbridge Rest Centre (Men's Institute)
(11th July 1944)

Babies a fortnight old in their mothers' arms and school children aged 8—10 were among 800 evacuees from London, who arrived at Chester Station on Tuesday 11th July accompanied by Salvation Army workers, school teachers and members of the WVS. They were taken by bus to prepared Rest Centres to be billeted in Chester, 200 for Handbridge.

'Evacuees do not want charity,' said the Town Clerk, 'we must provide accommodation and access to water and sanitary conveniences.'

Other services depend on the goodwill of the householder.

Chester Chronicle

Footnote:
Billeting was compulsory in Chester.

PHOTO—CHESTER CHRONICLE

▲ TOMMY HANDLEY, STAR OF THE RADIO PROGRAMME 'IT'S THAT MAN AGAIN', SIGNS AUTOGRAPHS FOR CHESTER CHILDREN 4TH SEPTEMBER, 1944
LEN MORGAN IS ON THE LEFT WITH CAP

6th June Invasion of Europe Launched
D-Day landings in Normandy.
New Ration Books issued in Handbridge schools.

Chester Chronicle, 10th June

15th July Second War-time Regatta; Colourful Scenes on the Dee

The Royal Navy, Western Command and RAF, Shrewsbury and King's Schools, Manchester and Leeds Universities co-operate with the wartime Federation of Chester Rowing Clubs to repeat last year's successful Regatta and Swimming Gala in aid of the British Red Cross PoWs. Thousands throng both banks of the River Dee to cheer the keenly contested swimming and sculling events. The Band of the Royal Marines provides musical interludes.

'EVERY MORNING, AT 7:15 PRECISELY, A LYSANDER WOULD DROP THE MAIL OVER WESTERN COMMAND HQ. WE SCHOOLBOYS WERE OFTEN LATE FOR SCHOOL WATCHING IT.' (LEN MORGAN)

NAAFI CLUB, LOVE STREET
(AFTER THE WAR, A CAFÉ AND FURNITURE STORE, NOW A RESTAURANT)
EXTENSIVELY USED BY SERVICE PERSONNEL OF WESTERN COMMAND

ANNEXE OF DEVA 'EMERGENCY' HOSPITAL, LIVERPOOL ROAD OPENED 1940 FOR WOUNDED AT DUNKIRK. MANY HANDBRIDGE GIRLS JOINED THE VAD. PHOTOGRAPH GIVEN TO LEN MORGAN BY LINDA ELLEY (2ND RIGHT)

42, EATON AVENUE WHERE A BOMB DAMAGED THE PEBBLEDASH. THE BOMB LANDED IN THE GARDEN OF Nº 48

A V.E. DAY ANNIVERSARY PARTY WAS HELD AT THE GROSVENOR ARMS ON 5TH MAY 1995 COMPLETE WITH CELEBRATORY CAKE.

DURING WORLD WAR II, A STICK OF BOMBS WAS DROPPED IN THE AREA. ONE BOMB FELL JUST BEYOND HERONBRIDGE. THE CRATER IN THE FIELD STILL EXISTS.

Flashback — St Mary's on-the-Hill

The Old Churchyard is full of gravestones of NCOs and men of the various regiments who died, while stationed at the adjacent Castle.

'Underneath lieth the remains of William Owens who served his King and Country faithfully as a NCO for 16 years in the ROYAL WELCH FUSILIERS. He departed this life 11th November 1834 Aged 47 years.'

'Here lies a true soldier whom all must applaud;

Many hardships he suffered at home and abroad:

But the hardest Engagement he ever was in

Was the Battle of Self in the Conquest of Sin.'

Victory in Europe (V.E.) Day—8th May 1945

'Cheshire can be justly proud of the contribution on the Home Front made for the War Effort,' wrote the Chester Chronicle on 12th May, announcing the end of the War in Europe (the defeat of Japan had to wait until 11th August). Men and women in the factories, farmers, farm workers and others of many occupations can look back with pride on the way they adapted themselves to war conditions. Cheshire, for example, a dairy farming county, switched to food production with tractors becoming almost as important as dairy cows and with the Land Army playing a prominent part. It was an exception not to have at least one of these green-jerseyed girls on a farm.

Handbridge joined the celebrations with welcome-home parties for returning service personnel and flags, bunting and street parties for children. One such was held in Mill Street with sports and games after tea. There was dancing in the street and pubs were thronged with customers.

PHOTO—CHESTER CHRONICLE

▲ V.E. DAY STREET PARTY IN GREENWAY STREET, MAY 1945 (NOTE AIR RAID SHELTER, RIGHT)

While everyone was celebrating V.E. Day in the UK, Cpl George Meredith, the father of Martin Meredith of 69 Hartington Street, was celebrating in Belgium at Talbot House (TocH), Poperinge. During the Great War, Talbot House was a rest centre and chapel behind the Ypres salient, used by thousands of soldiers on their way to battle. Today, it is the centre of the TocH movement for peace and a museum much visited by touring parties.

PHOTO—MARTIN MEREDITH

▲ V.E. DAY BEHIND TALBOT HOUSE, POPERINGE
CPL GEORGE ARTHUR MEREDITH (TOP, 2ND LEFT)
CELEBRATES WITH HIS REME PALS

PHOTO—NOEL ST JOHN WILLIAMS

▲ TALBOT HOUSE (TOCH) UPSTAIRS CHAPEL
'IN A MAD WORLD, AN OASIS OF PEACE'

Victory Celebrations

PHOTO—CHESTER CHRONICLE

KING GEORGE VI AND QUEEN ELIZABETH VISIT CHESTER ON 17TH JULY 1946, DURING THEIR CHESHIRE TOUR, TO THANK CITIZENS FOR THEIR PATRIOTIC SERVICE DURING THE WAR - SEEN HERE LEAVING THE TOWN HALL FOR A CATHEDRAL SERVICE.

Rifleman Keith Sarson KRRC, son of Canon and Mrs A W Sarson, St Mary's Rectory, was one of the first soldiers to return home. He was captured in the defence of Calais in 1940 and was rescued by the Americans from a PoW camp and flown home to join the celebrations

St Mary's Parish Magazine (August 1946)

On the occasion of the recent Royal Visit to Chester, to thank the people for their War Effort, St Mary's bellringers assisted at the Cathedral, where their Majesties spoke to some of them. King George and Queen Elizabeth were particularly interested in the fact that we had lady bellringers. The Queen asked Miss Hazel Close if she found bell-ringing difficult, while the King admitted that he had not previously met with lady campanologists.

The funeral took place on 28th August 1992 at Chester Crematorium of Mr John Evan Davies (72) of 87 Prenton Place, Handbridge. Mr Davies served in the RAF during World War II and was an ex-Battle of Britain fighter pilot. He was awarded five bravery medals including the Distinguished Flying Cross (DFC).

11th Aug 1945   V.J. Day

There were similar scenes of popular rejoicing, thanksgiving services in churches, parades and people making a 'night out', when the victory over Japan was announced. There was a bonfire and fireworks on 'Eagle's Eye' and St Mary's bellringers rang a peal. Many pubs ran dry!

A Memory

At 8:15 am GMT on 6th August 1945, my eighth birthday, an American aircraft dropped an atom bomb on the Japanese city of Hiroshima. Seventy eight thousand people died immediately with many more dying later from the effects of radiation.

The bomb brought peace to the rest of the world but the shadow of its terrible mushroom cloud has hung over the world ever since!

Grahame Jones, Queen's Park

Handbridge Sports and Carnival Festival

On 11th August 1945, HQ Western Command Sports Stadium, Eaton Road, was the venue for the huge Handbridge Sports and Carnival Festival attended by over five thousand people.

In the morning a carnival procession paraded the Chester streets en-route for the stadium. An athletics meeting had been arranged for the afternoon. In addition there were fancy goods stalls and pony and donkey rides. After tea Modern and Old Tyme dancing to the bands of the Flint British Legion and the Eaton Hall Naval Cadets was arranged but this was unfortunately spoiled by heavy rain.

However, troupes of Morris dancers, jazz bands, Sunday and day school tableaux, decorated carts, prams, bicycles and motor cars paraded around the stadium to entertain the spectators and provide a spectacular end to a happy 'Welcome Home' event.

PHOTO—BETTY BROSTER WHO WAS ONE OF THE CHILDREN PRESENT

AMONG THE CHILDREN FROM ECCLESTON PRIMARY SCHOOL SHOWN HERE ARE: JANE HEASMAN (LEFT, FULL FACE); GILLIAN ? (TO THE RIGHT OF JANE); MONICA HAYNES (TO THE RIGHT OF GILLIAN); SYLVIA WRIGHT (FULL FACE, TO THE RIGHT OF MONICA); THE ARM OF THE TEACHER, MISS WILLIAMS, CAN BE SEEN POINTING.

◀ FIELD MARSHAL, THE VISCOUNT BERNARD MONTGOMERY OF ALAMEIN ACCOMPANIED BY GENERAL BRIAN HORROCKS VISITS THE OFFICER CADET TRAINING UNIT (OCTU) AT EATON HALL IN 1948

The Cost

COMMEMORATIVE PLAQUE IN ▶
ST MARY'S CHURCH

THE NEW CEMETERY, OVERLEIGH
▼ THE GRAVE OF A CZECH SOLDIER WHO DIED IN 1940.
BELOW RIGHT: THE GRAVES OF BRITISH AND COMMONWEALTH SOLDIERS.

PHOTO—IAN BIRCHENOUGH

THE CLOCK IN THIS TOWER WAS RESTORED IN MEMORY OF THE MEN OF THIS PARISH WHO GAVE THEIR LIVES IN THE WAR 1939-1945 GLORY BE TO GOD.

PHOTO—LEN MORGAN

PHOTO—IAN BIRCHENOUGH

5

PHOTO—LEN MORGAN

Work

&

Leisure

PHOTO—CHESTER CHRONICLE

STEEPLEJACKS
POINTING THE STONEWORK
ON ST MARY'S STEEPLE

KATIE SAUNDERS (AGED 17)
EX QUEEN'S PARK HIGH SCHOOL
CHESHIRE OARSWOMEN OF THE YEAR 2001
GB REPRESENTATIVE AT COUPE DE LA JEUNESSE 2001

At Work

Thomas Nicholls—Tobacco and Snuff Mills

ALL PHOTOGRAPHS FROM THE THOMAS NICHOLLS CATALOGUE COURTESY OF BERNARD POWELL

▲ LORRIES, LINED UP OUTSIDE THE FACTORY IN 1932, CARRIED A HAND-PAINTED IMAGE OF JOHN PEEL, THE TOBACCO COMPANY'S TRADE MARK

Young girls called tobacco squashers were employed. We used to watch these poor, half starved young things, the stench of tobacco clinging to them plodding to work over the Old Dee Bridge.'

Maud Botting

Maud was born (1904) 'in a small house, where the post office now stands.'

County Quest. Nov 1997

1780	Established in Handbridge
1885	Roman gold coin of Titus dug up in a drain to the Snuff Mill
1950	Destroyed by fire
1954	Sold to Imperial Tobacco
1960s	Salmon Leap Flats replaced the factory

TOBACCO PROCESSES
TOP—LEAF SAMPLING ROOM
MIDDLE—CUTTING TOBACCO
BOTTOM—SPINNING ROLL

PACKING ROOM

Swindley's Iron Works

JAMES SWINDLEY (SON)
(BORN 1874)

PHOTO—LEN MORGAN

EASTGATE CLOCK
(DESIGNED BY JOHN DOUGLAS)

JAMES SWINDLEY (SR: FATHER)
(1848—1917)

PHOTO—GWEN SHALLCROSS NÉE SWINDLEY

Both father and son worked on making the iron framework for the Eastgate clock which commemorates the Diamond Jubilee of Queen Victoria in 1897.

In 1881 (census), James (Sen.) aged 33 was living with his wife, Mary, five sons and a daughter in Eccleston as the village blacksmith. In 1901, he had moved to 24 Overleigh Road. He died, aged 69, at Chester Castle.

Swindleys made the wrought iron work in St Mary's Church designed by the Church's architect, Mr F B Wade.

PHOTO—GWEN SHALLCROSS NÉE SWINDLEY

SWINDLEY'S BLACKSMITH SHOP ▼

▲ JAMES SWINDLEY HARD AT WORK AT THE FORGE

PHOTO—GWEN SHALLCROSS NÉE SWINDLEY

THE IRONWORKS WERE FIRST REPLACED BY A PRINTING WORKS AND THEN BY TODAY'S ORTHODONTIST PRACTICE.▼
(NOTE THE SMOKE VENT STILL ON THE ROOF)

PHOTO—LEN MORGAN

PHOTO—LEN MORGAN

▲ H A CLEGG & SONS, MONUMENTAL MASONS REPLACED BY
STEVEN BLACKWELL, STONE CRAFT ▼

PHOTO—LEN MORGAN

PHOTO—LEN MORGAN

▲ JOHN SALISBURY, STONEMASON PUTS THE
FINISHING TOUCHES TO A HEADSTONE
MEMORIAL

▼ POINTING THE STONEWORK ON ST
MARY'S TOWER, 1971
CENTRE LEFT: CHARLIE TURNER
CENTRE RIGHT: JACK MASSEY

PHOTO—GILL SHONE (DAUGHTER OF JACK MASSEY)

The Rope Walk

Rope making was established in Overleigh Road well before 1810. The Rope Walk entrance was situated next door to the Red Lion (p. 28). It was the premises of Messrs Harkers (1880—1922), who produced ropes, twine, nets and brushes for the hardware trade. The site is now occupied by new housing, Overleigh Court.

FORMER STABLES OF HERBIE WILD
(C1930) IN GREENWAY STREET ▶

FAMILY PHOTOGRAPH

THESE STABLES WERE CONVERTED TO
AN OFFSET PRINTERS AND THEN
BECAME THE MEDICAL CENTRE IN
1989 ▼

PHOTO—LEN MORGAN

▼ 7/9 HANDBRIDGE, NUMARK PHARMACY OWNED BY
GORDON COUPER AND WILLIAM COULTER
IN 1946, THE PHARMACY WAS OWNED BY OWEN PRITCHARD MPS

PHOTO—LEN MORGAN

◀ CORONA POP WORKS 1958—STAFF ENJOYING A BREAK
ON THE LEFT IS PAT DURKIN AND NORMA BARROW.
CORONA WAS REPLACED BY A KWIK SAVE SUPERMARKET AND TODAY
BY THE ABBEYFIELD SHELTERED HOUSING

PHOTO—PAT DURKIN

HANDBRIDGE DENTAL PRACTICE, OPENED 1986
MISS JANET POTTER, OWNER AND DENTIST. THE PRACTICE IS A
MEMBER OF THE BRITISH DENTAL ASSOCIATION (BDA) GOOD
◀ PRACTICE SCHEME. ▼

PHOTO—JANET POTTER

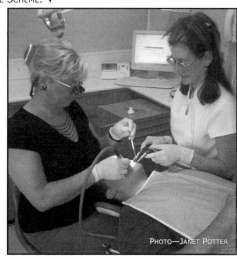

PHOTO—JANET POTTER

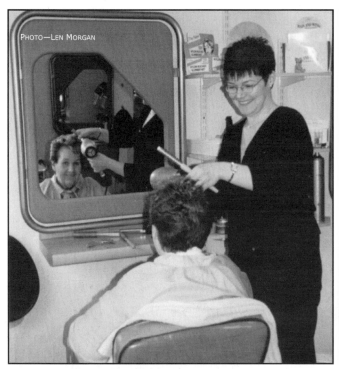

PHOTO—LEN MORGAN

▲ JULIE AT THE VOGUE HAIRDRESSING SALON

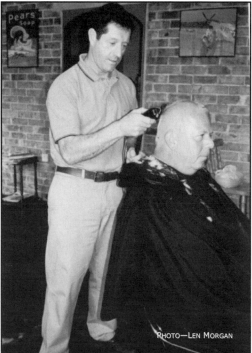

PHOTO—LEN MORGAN

▲ DAVE HURST FOLLOWING A FAMILY TRADITION, HERE GIVING JOHN SUTHERLAND HIS USUAL 'SHORT BACK AND SIDES'

GET ME TO THE RACE ON TIME

PHOTO—DAILY POST

FELICITY HAT HIRE, 18 HANDBRIDGE, WAS OWNED AND MANAGED BY JANET LEECH. BELOW, SHE MODELS A BROAD, BLACK SOMBRERO MADE FAMOUS BY ANDIE MACDOWELL IN 'FOUR WEDDINGS AND A FUNERAL' (JULY 1997). THE SHOP OPENED IN MAY 1995.

SUZANNE TATLER (LEFT), THE LANDLADY OF THE WHITE HORSE IN HANDBRIDGE, IS OFF TO 'LADIES DAY' AT CHESTER RACES IN A FELICITY HAT WHICH IS AN ACTUAL WORKING CLOCK.

PHOTO—LEN MORGAN

PHOTO—'IN BUSINESS' JULY 1997
COURTESY OF JANET LEECH

▲ THE LOCAL POST OFFICE AND SWEET SHOP MARGARET AND IAN JONES

Leisure Activities

A feature of 20th century Britain is the increase in leisure time available to employees. Legislation has given a shorter working day, freer weekends and annual holidays, confirmed by the Holidays with Pay Act of 1938. More free time has led to the development of leisure activities and tourism. Handbridge and Queen's Park possess two natural amenities—the River Dee and the surrounding green belt. These provide centres for sporting activities, river cruising, boating and rowing clubs. Opportunities for recreation have been increased for adults and schoolchildren by playing fields and playgrounds. Today, there are indoor facilities for entertainment and social gatherings. Cinemas, libraries and night-clubs are close by in Chester. TV is now a feature of most homes.

PHOTO—THE LATE SIDNEY VENO

▲ RIVER CRUISES TO THE IRON BRIDGE ON BITHELL'S BOATS WERE A POPULAR PASTIME (1920s)

1880	Bithell family first associated with boat hire on the River Dee
1938	Bithell Boats Ltd founded
1981	Bithell Company (original company) went into liquidation

PLEASURE CRUISE ADVERTISEMENTS FROM 1949
THE PICTURE SHOWS THE ECCLESTON FERRY
▼ (SEE NEXT PAGE)

▼ THE "VOLUNTEER" MOORED BY THE BANKS OF QUEEN'S PARK c1905
NOTE THE OLD SUSPENSION BRIDGE IN THE BACKGROUND

PHOTO—THE LATE SIDNEY VENO

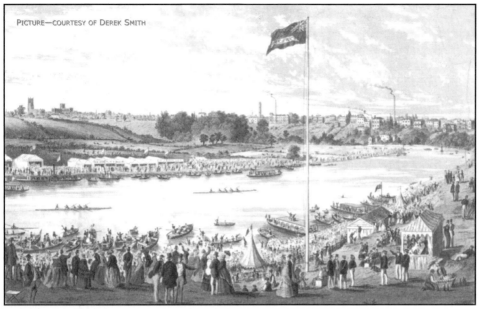

THIS VIEW OF THE RIVER DEE WAS TAKEN FROM THE SANDY LANE BANK AND SHOWS IN THE BACKGROUND FROM LEFT TO RIGHT:

ST JOHN'S CHURCH TOWER BEFORE IT COLLAPSED IN 1881;

CATHEDRAL;

LEADWORKS SHOT TOWER AND SANDOWN TERRACE;

RIVERSIDE HOUSING, BOUGHTON;

CHIMNEY OF THE WATERWORKS INTAKE AT BARRELWELL HILL

▲ CHESTER REGATTA 1854—BRITAIN'S OLDEST REGATTA
THE RACE FOR THE CHALLENGE CUP, GIFT OF EARL GROSVENOR MP, AND WON BY MANCHESTER (NEMESIS) ROWING CLUB

◄ THE ANNUAL RAFT RACE 1979
MEMBERS OF THE CREW OF HMS BROADSWORD (AFFILIATED TO CHESTER) HAVE FUN AT THE ANNUAL RAFT RACE IN 1979. HMS BROADSWORD WAS SOLD TO THE BRAZILIAN NAVY IN 1995

ECCLESTON FERRY c1908
THE CHAIN FERRY WAS BUILT BY WILLIAM ROBERTS, DESIGNER AND BUILDER OF STEAM LAUNCHES AND YACHTS, CRANE BANK, CHESTER. HE LIVED AT PYECROFT HOUSE (SEE P 155) AND WAS THE GREAT GRANDFATHER OF DILYS DOWSWELL

PHOTO—LEN MORGAN

▲ St Mary's Handbridge Cub Scout Summer Camp
July 1992—Brookside Farm Poulton. This field was the crash site of a Junkers 88 bomber during World War II

PHOTO—LEN MORGAN

▲ Cups won by St Mary's 18th Chester Scout Band
20th March 1993—Royal Albert hall

◀ Morris Dance Troop 1970
Rear, L to R:
Yvonne Bellis, (unknown), Susan Owen, Janette Turner, Sandra Fieldstead, Kim Shone, (unknown)
Front, L to R
Susan Morgan, Annie Ankers, Beth Johnson, Susan Liversage, Susan Turner

PHOTO—Chester Observer

▼ The "Kingy" Playing Field, Eaton Road June 1950

PHOTO—Pearl Evans

Rear L to R:
Pam Barwise, Pearl Day, Barbara Moore, Rita Starkey, Nora Hignett, Mary Walsh, A Briggs
Middle L to R
Kath Leonard, Mary Powis, Beryl Jackson, Pat Wilson, Mary Greatbanks
Front L to R
Pam Dean, Shirley Hull, Janet Mealing, Marian Hughes, Kath Price, Brenda Price, Sylvia Walters

The wooden Parish Hall once stood near this site note Netherfield House in the background

Boxing

PHOTO—JIM DAVIES

▲ BOXING MATCHES WERE A COMMON ENTERTAINMENT IN THE FIRST HALF OF THE CENTURY. SUCH FIGHTS TOOK PLACE BEHIND THE RED LION IN THE 1920S AND 1930S. THE REFEREE IN THE TOP HAT, JIMMY JONES AND HIS SONS, JOE AND JACK, (WITH TOWELS) ARE SHOWN IN THIS PHOTOGRAPH. THE FIGHTER ON THE LEFT IS BELIEVED TO BE EVAN TOTTY—THE ONE ON THE RIGHT IS UNKNOWN.

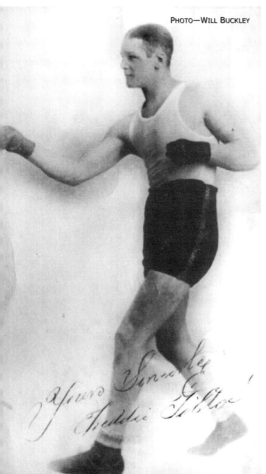

PHOTO—WILL BUCKLEY

◄ **FRED TILSTON** WAS BORN IN 1907 AND LIVED AT 5 EDGAR PLACE. HE WAS ONE OF TEN BROTHERS AND SISTERS. FRED ATTENDED HANDBRIDGE ST MARY'S CE SCHOOL AND, AT THE AGE OF 15, MADE HIS BOXING DEBUT AT THE LIVERPOOL STADIUM AS A PROFESSIONAL BOXER. AT THE AGE OF 21, HE WENT TO CANADA WHERE HE BECAME NATIONAL LIGHTWEIGHT CHAMPION. HE WAS THE UNCLE OF MRS PAULINE PRESCOTT, WIFE OF THE DEPUTY PRIME MINISTER.

JIMMY WALSH, BORN IN 1912, ALSO ATTENDED HANDBRIDGE ST MARY'S CE SCHOOL. HE BECAME A PROFESSIONAL BOXER, WINNING THE BRITISH LIGHTWEIGHT TITLE IN 1936 AT LIVERPOOL. HE IS BURIED IN OVERLEIGH NEW CEMETERY. THE INSCRIPTION ON HIS GRAVE READS 'SPORTSMAN OF THIS CITY'. THE FATHER OF IAN JONES (SEE PAGE 58) WHO KEPT THE JOLLY MILLER PUB (1960— 82) WAS ONE OF JIMMY WALSH'S SPARRING PARTNERS. ▶

PHOTO—CIGARETTE CARD

PHOTO—MAY MCHUGH (FATHER, TOP FAR RIGHT)

ST MARY'S AFC 1923 / 24 MANY HERE WOULD HAVE SERVED IN WORLD WAR I

PHOTO—JOHN GERRARD

BRICKFIELDS AFC—CHESTER – RUNCORN CUP (JUNIOR) 1923 / 24
BRICKFIELDS WON 6—0

BACK: W LLOYD, F PRICE, JOHN GERRARD, T DONE, HOULT, LEWIS, CROSSLEY
MIDDLE: D CHIME, A HOULT, J HOLYOAK, WAINWRIGHT   FRONT: JENKINS, DAIN, T JONES, HANMER, GORDON GUNSON

GREG MORRIS MEMORIAL
TROPHY MATCH
THE CATHOLIC HIGH SCHOOL
TEAM (JOHN ALEXANDER AND
ANDREW BYARD, FRONT)
PLAYED AT HANDBRIDGE IN A
CHARITY MATCH TO RAISE
MONEY FOR A MEMORIAL
TROPHY TO HONOUR THE
MEMORY OF GREG MORRIS
WHO DIED SUDDENLY AT THE
NORTHGATE ARENA

BRICKFIELDS FC TAKEN AT CITY HIGH SCHOOL FOR GIRLS, 1930
1ST RIGHT, FRONT ROW, SEATED IS CHARLIE LAYFIELD WHO LATER PLAYED FOR EVERTON AND WALES AND WAS MANAGER OF WREXHAM FC.
3RD RIGHT, FRONT ROW IS TOMMY JONES, IAN'S (PAGE 62) GRANDFATHER, NOTED FOR HIS BARE KNUCKLE BOXING. HE USED TO WALK TO
LIVERPOOL FOR HIS FIGHTS AND ON HIS WAY BACK SPENT HIS MONEY IN PUBS. WHAT HE HAD LEFT, HE DONATED TO HIS WIFE!

Some other Football notables:

Eric Lee: former City Grammar School pupil, lived in Appleyards Lane, played as an amateur for Chester FC in 3rd Division North (1946—57) and for Great Britain in 1948 Olympics.

Trevor Walters: from Greenway Street, played for Chester FC and Wales.

Billy Foulkes: married a Handbridge girl (née Cheers from Meadows Lane), played for Chester FC, Newcastle and Wales. Played in the 1952 Cup Final for Newcastle United

Alan Tarbuck, Brian Woodall, Paul Hallows and Graham Pugh: former Overleigh Secondary Modern schoolboys who played for Chester Schoolboys and then turned professional for Chester and Everton (Alan), Sheffield Wednesday (Brian and Graham) and Bolton (Paul).

PHOTO—JOHN TOMLINSON

HANDBRIDGE MEN'S
INSTITUTE FC IN 1950S ▶
SECTION 'C' WINNERS /
McDERMOTT CUP WINNERS

BACK L TO R:
 J WESTWATER, R THOMAS,
 T HUGHES, F NICHOLSON,
 G FARRINGTON, G WESTWATER

FRONT (SEATED) L TO R:
 HERBIE FIELDSTEAD,
 J TOMLINSON, LES WARD,
 B CLARKE, F PEERS

Handbridge Cricket Club

PHOTO—GORDON STODDART

◀ 1936
BACK L TO R:
 C EVANS, B STURLEY, J POWELL,
 D CHIMES, G THOMAS, A BLAKE,
 W MOORCROFT, MR STURLEY

FRONT (SEATED) L TO R:
 D CROSSLEY, F DAVIES,
 G GUNSON (CAPT), W HANMER,
 L HOLLAND (LANDLORD OF THE
 CARLTON TAVERN)

PHOTO—GORDON STODDART

1939—WINNERS OF BOUGHTON
HALL KNOCK-OUT COMPETITION ▶
BACK L TO R:
 A DONOVAN, H SMITH, H SIMMS,
 REV A ABBOT, G GUNSON (CAPT),
 H PRATT, B POWELL

FRONT L TO R:
 J POWELL, F WARD, H POWELL,
 L HOLLAND

Affectionately known as 'The Club' ....

Around 1887, a Mr Bulkley Jacson settled in Curzon Park: he was interested in the welfare of young men and the provision of organised recreation for them. Beside the Coach and Horses Inn in Handbridge, was a Court which housed a dame school, before the advent of compulsory school education (1870). Mr Jacson hired this room, installed heat and lighting so that youths could enjoy indoor games in comfort. 'So popular was the venture, that he engaged premises in Pyecroft Street and established, with a committee, *The Young Men's Friendly Society* for boys of 14 and over.'
St Mary's Parochial Council 1964. *A Handbridge Miscellany.*

Billiards and bagatelle were played on the ground floor, while upstairs there was a room for lectures, concerts and a small library. Outdoor games were played on a field in Eaton Road shared with the King's School. A river trip to Eccleston Ferry in a hired barge attracted the attention of the Duke who, invited to see the activities at Pyecroft Street, decided to build the Men's Institute and present this amenity to the community to enhance the social life of the district.

▼ CELEBRATING THE 75TH ANNIVERSARY OF THE INSTITUTE IN 1970
IN THE CENTRE IS MRS EDWARDS AND BEHIND HER, HER HUSBAND, LEN, THE CHEMIST.

PHOTO—MARTIN MEREDITH

PHOTO—DON SCARL

HANDBRIDGE MEN'S INSTITUTE SNOOKER TEAMS
WINNERS, TEMPERANCE LEAGUE AND CUP, 1ST DIVISION 1963
CHAMPIONS 2ND DIVISION, CHESTER & DISTRICT LEAGUE 1964 OBSERVER
SHIELD (SHOWN)
BACK: GEORGE THOMAS, BARRIE HIPKISS, TONY ALLEN, DON SCARL
FRONT: ALLEN TOMLINSON, BRIAN HUGHES, JACK BRENNAN

St Mary's Infant School 1941—6

As 5 and 6 year old boys and girls, we used to go across the road to the Handbridge Men's Institute to dance to records and the piano upstairs in the large hall.

We used to receive a half bottle of milk every day to drink. During holidays, a crate of milk and box of straws were left on the steps of the old Parish Hall . We would go and drink our milk and replace the empty bottles in the crate and the used straws in a dustbin—no vandalism and no taking more than one bottle! Can you imagine that happening today?

Don Scarl

Pageants, Parties and Personalities

Events

It is hardly surprising that Handbridge, with its historic and picturesque river, its extensive green fields and its churches and schools should be a popular venue for celebrating national and local occasions with pageants, carnivals, fêtes and street parties.

The Maypole and Mayday Revels

The finding, erecting and decoration of the maypole was an important part of community life every May Day from the 14th century. The maypole was also the focal point for village dancing, the crowning of the May Queen and the celebration of the Spring season.

PICTURE—O.U.P.

PICTURE—JAMES WILLIAMS, THE STORY OF CHESTER. 1900

PHOTO—CHESTER OBSERVER

▲ CELEBRATING THE CORONATION OF KING EDWARD VII
9TH AUGUST 1902, OUTSIDE HANDBRIDGE MEN'S INSTITUTE
THIS WAS THE SPOT AT THE JUNCTION OF EATON AND OVERLEIGH ROADS, WHERE THE MAYPOLE HAD STOOD SINCE MEDIEVAL TIMES

Maypole Ceremony, Handbridge, 25th June 1902

At 6:15 pm on Wednesday, 25th June, 100 children assembled on the spot on which the Maypole stands, just within the enclosure of the Handbridge Men's Institute. In ideal weather, witnessed by a large crowd of spectators, including the Rector, Rev H Grantham and daughter Gwynedd, the Sheriff (R Cecil Davies) and Alderman and Mrs George Dutton, the children danced around the historic Maypole. Suitably painted with Grosvenor colours (yellow and black) and decked with laurels etc., the Maypole looked very pretty and brought to the minds of older inhabitants, the many dances they had witnessed in days gone by. The children were trained by the schoolmaster and schoolmistress, Mr and Mrs R Atherton. Mr G Parker supplied the Pole and Mr J Swindley the ironwork.

In perfect weather, five hundred children and five hundred adults saw Miss Margaret Davies crowned St Mary's Queen of the May. She addressed her subjects in verse:

> *Greetings fair subjects whom around I see,*
>
> *And thank you for the honour now bestowed on me.*
>
> *May real blessings all your lives endower,*
>
> *Who live beneath St Mary's noble Tower*

In bygone days, where the Men's Institute now stands, was a public house known as The Maypole [later the Old House at Home]. There each May Day in Mediæval times, the maypole was danced around. It became a permanent fixture, until removed on 27th June 1850. Twenty six years later, when the Rev H Grantham was rector of St Mary's Church, a revival was held. Another lapse followed until this year, when the Rev A W Sarson resurrected the Maypole dancing. Now, he wants to make the event permanent.

5th May 1928
Chester Chronicle, founded 1775

MISS MARGARET DAVIES AGED 13 IN 1928 ▼

PHOTO—MR S SHONE

MAYPOLE DANCING 1949. ST MARY'S FÊTE ON THE RECTORY LAWN ▼

PHOTO—CHESTER CHRONICLE

3000 PERFORMERS

AND

4000 SEATS DAILY.

2/-, 3/6, 5/-, 7/6
10/6, & £1 1s.

UNDER
ROYAL
PATRONAGE.

CHESTER
Historical Pageant

JULY 18th till 23rd, 1910,

At 2-45 p.m. Daily.

Patrons :
T.R.H. THE PRINCE AND PRINCESS OF WALES.
T.S.H. THE DUKE AND DUCHESS OF TECK.

President :
HIS GRACE THE DUKE OF WESTMINSTER.
(LORD LIEUTENANT OF THE COUNTY.)

President of the Ladies' Committee :
HER GRACE THE DUCHESS OF WESTMINSTER.

Vice-Presidents :
THE MARCHIONESS OF CHOLMONDELEY.
THE COUNTESS OF STAMFORD.

PHOTO—HERITAGE CENTRE CR169/23

▲ ADVERTISEMENT FOR THE PAGEANT
'THE PAGEANT WAS HELD ON SOME OF THE GOOD FAT ACRES THAT HUGH LUPUS WON
WITH HIS SWORD' (OFFICIAL PROGRAMME) NOW THE PLAYING FIELDS OPPOSITE
GREENBANK (STILL KNOWN LOCALLY AS THE PAGEANT FIELD)

▲ MRS RUTH CHARINGTON AS 'DEVA'
FROM A COLLECTION GIVEN BY MRS M EDGE OF
HANDBRIDGE AND NOW ON THE CHH'S IMAGEBANK

▼ EPISODE I—AGRICOLA, THE ROMAN GOVERNOR OF BRITAIN, RETURNS TO DEVA AFTER DEFEATING THE ORDOVICES AD 78

PHOTO—CHESTER CITY LIBRARY

EPISODE II—KING EDGAR RECEIVES HOMAGE cAD 873
THIS EPISODE REPRESENTS THE POPULAR LEGEND OF EIGHT TRIBUTARY KINGS ROWING KING EDGAR ON THE DEE cAD 873. WHILE THE CHILDREN FORM THE RIVER BANKS, KING EDGAR IS MET BY THE SAXON POPULACE AND NOBILITY

Spectacular Pageant in Handbridge

A field opposite Green Bank provided the arena for Chester's Historical Pageant 1910. The Pageant Field seated 4 000 with room for another 6 000 standing.

"In front of the grandstand lies the beautiful green glade with its dark background of woodland foliage—an ideal setting for the Chester Pageant in eight episodes. Through artificial portals, erected along the hedgerows, enters a myriad of children dressed in brilliant colours—fairies entering a dream world for the opening ceremony."

Later the children returned to form the banks of the River Dee, along which the legendary eight tributary kings rowed King Edgar down the river (Episode II).

The first of the historical episodes illustrated the Roman occupation of the City. Priestesses attended the altar as Agricola led his noble train of tribunes, trumpeters, standard bearers and legionaries of the victorious XX and II Legions.

Episode followed episode, introducing kings and queens, princesses and prelates, mailed knights and noble ladies, Saxon warriors, Cheshire bowmen and wild Welshmen in a blaze of colour and action to thrill the citizens and visitors.

The Pageant ended with King Charles I watching the Battle of Rowton Moor from the City Walls. A wounded Cavalier brought the news of the defeat of his army and fell dead at his feet. Leaving the City to its fate, the King rode out of the arena and turned his horse towards the road to North Wales (Overleigh Road) and his eventual execution.

Based on Chester Chronicle report July 1910

EPISODE VIIb: MIDSUMMER REVELS ABOUT 1620 AD

These Revels were held in earlier times on Midsummer's Eve or Day but, after the Restoration of Charles II (1660), they were held on 29th May. Episode VIIb depicts Chester keeping holiday in 1620 (reign of James I & VI), led by the 25 City Guilds, who loved processions, show, pantomime and simple dance in the open air.

PHOTO—CHESTER CITY LIBRARY

PHOTO—CHESTER CITY LIBRARY

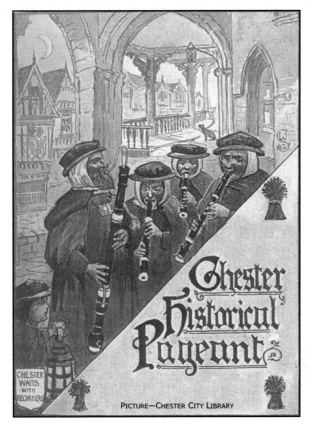

CHESTER WAITS WITH RECORDERS

PICTURE—CHESTER CITY LIBRARY

▲ ▲ MAYPOLE DANCING

▲ THE CHOIR WITH CONDUCTOR, DR BRIDGE, ORGANIST OF CHESTER CATHEDRAL

◄ CHESTER WAITS—THE COVER OF THE BOOK OF MUSIC, EDITED BY DR JOSEPH C BRIDGE, WHO COMPOSED, ARRANGED AND SELECTED ALL THE PAGEANT MUSIC.

The Revels opened with a Maypole dance to the tune *'Come, lasses and lads'* sung by the choir under its conductor, Dr Bridge. A Morris dance and a dance by the Dairy Maids followed. The Maypole ribbons were unfurled to a song by the choir and danced by the Elves and Fairies. The Episode ended with the Charge of the Hobby Horses, the antics of a Merry Andrew, and the procession of the animals (elephant, camel, ass, unicorn etc) and the Guild Boys carrying banners.

> *"This Episode was acknowledged by the world's press as the finest and most successful of the whole series."*
>
> Frank Simpson,
> Hon Secretary,
> Performers' Committee
>
> (Chester City Library)

PHOTO—HILARY THOMAS (DAUGHTER OF NELLIE PARKER)

▲ MISS VICTORIA ELLEN (NELLIE) PARKER AGED 12, A MAYPOLE DANCER IN EPISODE VII (1898—1999). SHE WAS EDUCATED AT THE CITY AND COUNTY SCHOOL FOR GIRLS AND CREWE TEACHER TRAINING COLLEGE, LATER TEACHING IN CHESTER SCHOOLS INCLUDING LOVE STREET. SHE WAS THE MOTHER OF HILARY THOMAS WHO ATTENDED THE CITY HIGH SCHOOL FROM 1944 TO 1951.

RIGHT AND BELOW:
1) SIR GEOFFREY SHAKERLEY, EP.VIII, (MAJOR G SHAKERLEY)
2) KNIGHTS PASSING UNDER THE BRIDGEGATE EN ROUTE FOR THE ARENA
3) ERMENTRUDE, COUNTESS OF CHESTER, EP.III, (LADY ARTHUR GROSVENOR)
4) BISHOP OF WINCHESTER, EP.VII, (REV H GRANTHAM)
5) KING EDGAR, EP. II (THE MAYOR OF CHESTER, ALD. D L HEWITT)

PHOTO—CHESTER CITY LIBRARY

PHOTO—HERITAGE CENTRE CR453, COURTESY OF MRS EDGE

PHOTO—CHESTER CITY LIBRARY

PHOTO—CHESTER CITY LIBRARY

PHOTO—CHESTER CITY LIBRARY

Chester's Historic Pageant 1937

Chester celebrated the Coronation of King George VI with a Pageant on the College grounds and an illuminated Tattoo on the River Dee.

Handbridge

The Parish of Handbridge was given the responsibility for Episode IV:

The Founding of the Abbey of Saint Werburgh AD 1093 by Hugh Lupus.
(Chairman: Rev A W Sarson MA)

Theme of Episode IV

William the Conqueror largely replaced the local Anglo-Saxon lords by earls of his choosing, who 'subdued by the sword'. One of these, Hugh of Avranches (Hugh Lupus, the Wolf) succeeded Gerbod the Fleming to become the second Earl of Chester. At the instigation of his friend, Anselm, Abbot of Bec (later to become Archbishop of Canterbury), Hugh founded the great Abbey of St Werburgh, which was to become Chester Cathedral.

Searchlight Military Tattoo

WILL TAKE PLACE ON
THE PAGEANT GROUND

Highwayman Episode by The Cheshire Yeomanry.

Fighting with Quarterstaffs

Trooping the Colour

The Band of The King's Shropshire Light Infantry.

Great Historical Finale by Depot, Cheshire Regiment.

SCENES AND TABLEAUX by Boy's Brigade.

PATRIOTIC SCENE by 200 Girl Guides.

HEALTH AND FITNESS EXERCISES by members of the Women's League of Health and Beauty.

FOLK DANCING by members of English Folk Dancing Society.

100 THRILLS A MINUTE by members of the Motorcycle Club.

CLASSICAL DANCING by Miss Hammond's Students.

FAIRY PLAYS by Miss C Kendrick's School of Dancing.

WESTMINSTER SMARTER FIRE BRIGADE

CESTRIAN TOREADORS

PRICES (inc Tax) 2/6, 1/6, 1/-

Searchlight Tattoo

'The centre piece of the week was the Illuminated River Pageant with a great display of Fireworks on the Meadows. Thousands lined both banks of the Dee to watch the display. The Suspension Bridge glittered in red, white and blue, and a long chain of lights stretched round the loop of the river, while houses and gardens on both sides of the Dee were lit up.'

Chester Chronicle

'The Chester Diocesan Guild of Church Bellringers rang a peal of 'Kent Treble Bob Major' with 5088 changes at St Mary's Church in 3 hours 20 minutes.'

'The residents of Brown's Lane and their children were entertained to tea in an adjoining field. Sixty children and parents then enjoyed a sports competition at which the Rev J Abbott, minister of the Handbridge Congregational Church, presided.'

Chester Chronicle

'We are grateful to the Radio Department of Brown's of Chester for making it possible for the Coronation Ceremonies to be relayed in St Mary's Church.'

Parish Magazine
June 1937

▼ HUGH LUPUS IS REPROVED BY ANSELM, ABBOT OF BEC, FOR HIS MANY MISDEEDS

PHOTO—OFFICIAL PROGRAMME. CHESTER CITY LIBRARY

Celebrations

The Coronation of King George V and Queen Mary, 22nd June 1911

After the short reign of King Edward VII, King George V was crowned in Westminster Abbey 'amid a scene of gorgeous pomp'. Chester was a blaze of colour to mark the occasion.

In the suburbs, in every back and side street, flags, bunting and streamers were to be seen galore. Scarcely a house was without its Union Jack or Picture in its windows. At the King's request, all schools had been granted a week's holiday.

The River Dee was illuminated and the King Edgar River Pageant was revived from the 1910 Pageant.

The King was rowed up the Dee by the eight Tributary Kings. The procession of the Saxon monarch and his illuminated boats and steamers was an exaggeration but a pardonable twist of history!

Chester Chronicle 24th June 1911

King George V Jubilee, 1935

▲ CHILDREN FROM MEADOW LANE JOINED THOSE FROM APPLEYARDS LANE AND PRENTON PLACE TO ENJOY A PARTY TO CELEBRATE THE JUBILEE OF KING GEORGE V

▲ ALLINGTON PLACE CELEBRATING THE JUBILEE OF KING GEORGE V

Queen Victoria's Coronation (29th June 1838) Remembered

10,000 in Procession through Chester led by Local Sunday School Children

3000 schoolchildren marched to the Linen Hall, where a sumptuous entertainment awaited them. The board was graced by 120 joints of meat weighing 1800 lbs, 218 plum puddings weighing about 1526 lbs, bread, potatoes served up cold and, despite a teetotal protest, some very creditable small beer.

The children were cleared away by 2 o'clock: by 3 o'clock, more than 1000 labouring men were ranged round the same board and were served with 1000 lbs weight of roast beef, bread etc and 700 lbs of plum pudding. They were carved by the gentry and tradesmen 'and all seemed happy and contented'.

Handbridge
At Eaton all the labourers employed in 'the vast demesne' were regaled at the cost of the Noble Marquis.

The children in the various schools in the neighbourhood had a holiday, medals were distributed to them and other means of enjoying and commemorating the day provided.

Chester Chronicle 19th May 1937

Celebration of VE Day, 8th May 1945

Festival of Britain 1951

PHOTO—GILLIAN BROWN

PHOTO—GILLIAN BROWN

PHOTO—COURTESY OF MRS MAY MORETON

▲ VICTORY IN EUROPE (VE) DAY PARTY

◄ VICTORY IN JAPAN (VJ) DAY PARTY

BEESTON PATHWAY, HANDBRIDGE

▲ WHILE THE PEOPLE OF BRITAIN CELEBRATED THE END OF AUSTERITY, HANDBRIDGE CONGREGATIONAL CHURCH APPOINTED ITS OWN FESTIVAL QUEEN— PAM JONES (NÉE MOORE)

The Coronation of Queen Elizabeth II, 2nd June 1953

Handbridge joined the nation in celebrating the coronation of Queen Elizabeth II on 2nd June 1953 with church services, parties for young and old in gaily decorated streets, while many watched the ceremony on TV or listened on the radio.

Greenway Street had its own party and Coronation Queen and celebrated the occasion on the banks of the Dee.

PHOTO—COURTESY OF MRS MAY MORETON

▲ GREENWAY STREET CELEBRATING CORONATION DAY ON THE BANKS OF THE RIVER DEE
THE GUEST OF HONOUR WAS THE CORONATION QUEEN, MARGARET WILLIAMS.
MRS MORETON, WHO SUPPLIED THE PHOTOGRAPH, IS SHOWN, FRONT ROW, THIRD FROM THE RIGHT IN THE LIGHT OVERCOAT.

PHOTO—COURTESY OF MRS MAY MORETON

CORONATION PARTY, GREENWAY STREET, 2ND JUNE 1953
MARGARET WILLIAMS (15) OF 5 GREENWAY STREET WAS CHOSEN CORONATION QUEEN

◄ QUEEN MARGARET CROWNED BY MRS G B JACKSON
L TO R: PAM MOORE, PAT MORTON, BARBARA GERRARD, MRS JACKSON, MARGARET WILLIAMS, BARBARA ASHLEY, JOSIE RANDLES, BARBARA MOORE
SEATED: JOEY JOHNSON, JENNIFER BUCKLEY

PHOTO—COURTESY OF MRS MAY MORETON

Other Coronation parties were celebrated in Prenton Place/Appleyards Lane and Meadows Lane.
Observer June 1953

MARGARET TOURS HER KINGDOM ON THE DEE ►
L TO R
FRONT : BARBARA GERRARD, JOEY JOHNSON,
PAM MOORE
CENTRE: MARGARET WILLIAMS
BACK: BARBARA MOORE, PAT MORTON,
BARBARA ASHLEY, JOSIE RANDLES

Silver Jubilee of Queen Elizabeth II

PHOTO—LEN MORGAN

◄ SILVER JUBLILEE CELEBRATIONS IN PERCY ROAD, 2ND JUNE 1977
L TO R
FRONT: DAVID AND JOAN MORGAN
BACK: SUE, LIZ AND PETER MORGAN

PHOTO—RON TAYLOR

THE SILVER JUBILEE PARTY (1977) ►
IN PRENTON PLACE

Eaton Hall Officer Cadet Training Unit

In 1941, when the Royal Naval College, Dartmouth was bombed, the training of officers for the Royal Navy was moved to Eaton Hall, vacated by the Duke of Westminster to help the war effort.

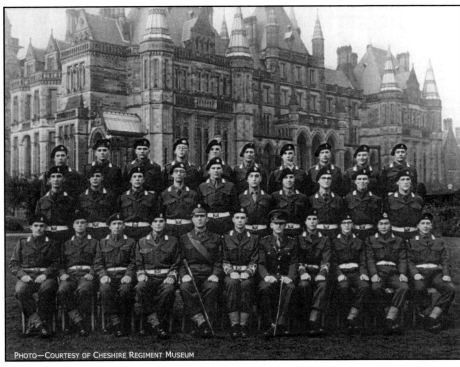

PHOTO—COURTESY OF CHESHIRE REGIMENT MUSEUM

▲ 164 OFFICER CADET TRAINING UNIT, EATON HALL, 1954 IN THEIR OFF-DUTY UNIFORMS WITH DISTINCTIVE WHITE COLLAR 'TABS'. THE OFFICER CADETS WERE A FAMILIAR SIGHT IN HANDBRIDGE.

In 1946 the Army still needed facilities for training National Service officers. Lt Gen Sir Brian Horrocks, General Officer Commanding in Chief, Western Command HQ in Chester moved 164 OCTU from North Wales to the vacant Eaton Hall. From 1946 to 1958 15000 National Service cadets were trained there.

The Queen's Visit - 1957

PHOTO—COURTESY OF MRS LIZA MOORE

As the Queen passed down Eaton Road, the school lined the road, eagerly waiting for the Royal car. We were so keen to get a really good view of her that we forgot to cheer!

Margaret Ginger, Form IV, City High School for Girls

The Inkwell, 1951

▲ QUEEN ELIZABETH II EN ROUTE TO EATON HALL AFTER PRESENTING NEW COLOURS TO THE CHESHIRE REGIMENT IN 1957. THE QUEEN IS SEEN TRAVELLING UP HANDBRIDGE PAST THE JUNCTION WITH QUEEN'S PARK VIEW.
ON A SIMILAR VISIT ON 28TH APRIL 1951, BUT AS PRINCESS ELIZABETH, SHE TOOK THE SALUTE AT THE PASSING OUT PARADE, 164 OCTU, EATON HALL, AND MET 400 CADETS, STAFF AND THEIR FAMILIES

Great Fires

J Nichols & Sons Tobacco and Snuff Factory: 21st June 1950

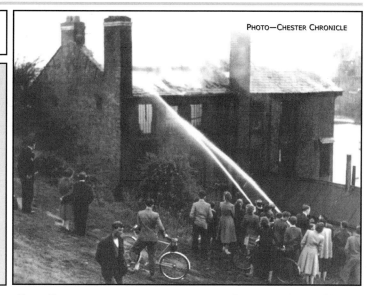

PHOTO—CHESTER CHRONICLE

A cigarette butt the cause of the Tobacco Mill Blaze? £12,000 damage

Smoke was first noticed by Gordon Sands, 24, Bradford Street, Handbridge, who was fishing in the Dee with some friends just below the Mill. So excited was he that, as he called out 'Fire!', he dropped a fish, that he had just caught, back into the river.

Chester Chronicle, 24th June 1950

THE DEMISE OF J NICHOLS & SONS TOBACCO AND SNUFF FACTORY ON THE BANKS OF THE RIVER. ESTABLISHED IN 1780, THE MILLS PROVIDED EMPLOYMENT FOR MANY MEN AND WOMEN IN HANDBRIDGE

Fire at Moore & Brocks Building Suppliers: 30th March 1988

MOORE & BROCKS HAD RUN A BUILDING SUPPLIERS YARD BEHIND THE GARAGE IN THE CENTRE OF HANDBRIDGE SINCE 1932. SHORTLY AFTER MOVING TO LARGER PREMISES, THE BUILDING WAS SET ALIGHT IN A SPECTACULAR FASHION ON 30TH MARCH 1988.
THE LAND HAD BEEN SOLD AS A SITE FOR SHELTERED HOUSING DEVELOPMENT.

PHOTO—LEN MORGAN

The empty building had become 'an adventure playground for local children'.

Police are believed to be looking for three children. Local Press

PHOTO—LEN MORGAN

IN THE SEVERE WINTER OF
1962—63, THE RIVER DEE FROZE
OVER FOR MANY WEEKS

PHOTO—HERITAGE CENTRE. CH0374

PHOTO—CHESTER CHRONICLE

PHOTO—LEN MORGAN

PHOTO—LEN MORGAN

PETER MORGAN ON THE LITTLE ROODEE AMONGST THE
BLOCKS OF ICE FROM THE FILTER BEDS AT THE WATER
WORKS, WHICH WERE LEFT THERE TO MELT

AN INTREPID MOTORCYCLIST AND PASSENGER BRAVE THE
FROZEN RIVER ON A TRIUMPH 3TA TWENTY-ONE

PHOTO—CHESTER CHRONICLE

THE DEE FROZE MANY TIMES DURING THIS CENTURY; 1906, 1910, 1917, 1929, 1947 AND 1962, FOR EXAMPLE.
THIS PHOTOGRAPH WAS TAKEN IN THE WINTER OF 1962/63

Patron: The Mayor of Chester, Councillor Lt. Col. H. A. Howell M.B.E., Admiral of the Dee, of 8 Queen's Park Road Handbridge.

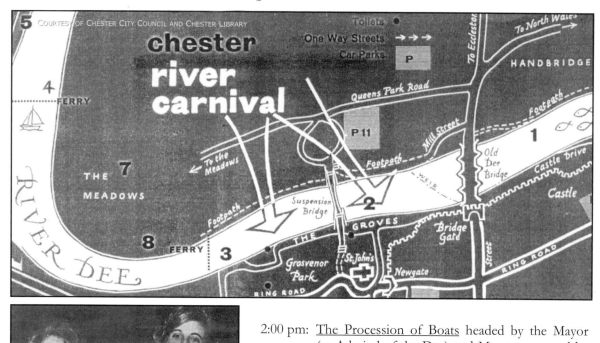

2:00 pm: <u>The Procession of Boats</u> headed by the Mayor (as Admiral of the Dee) and Mayoress, rowed by Sea Cadets. The Mayor will be piped ashore at the Groves. In the last boat will be the River Carnival Queen, Miss Gaynor Paddock and her attendants.

2:45 pm: Coracle Race; Canoe Obstacle Race; Greasy Pole; Sailing Dinghy Capsize; Rescue by RAF Helicopter; Fire Service Display; Hovercraft Demonstration.

   <u>Demonstration of Salmon Netting by Handbridge Fishermen</u>

Dusk: Procession of Illuminated Boats; Water Ballet by Sailing Dinghies at the Ford.

   In the nearby Meadows: a Barbecue (Chester Round Table for Charity); Firework Display by Brocks.

MISS CHRISTINE ANDREWS (MAID OF HONOUR) AND MISS GAYNOR PADDOCK (RIVER QUEEN)

> *Fun and games at the River Carnival before a crowd of 25 000*
> *'Bogus' Mayor thrown into the Dee.*
> *First River Carnival after a lapse of 30 years.*
> *Splendid show as 32 boats and 27 other craft sail in procession.*
>
> Chester Observer

PHOTO—PAT CLEAVER (DAUGHTER)

ALFRED 'JIM' CLEAVER

Gallantry Medal for Policeman

In February 1934 Constable Alfred Cleaver of Eaton Road, Handbridge, was presented with the King's Medal for Gallantry at an Investiture at Buckingham Palace by King George V. In January 1933, he and Sergeant Capper entered a 'blazing inferno' three times in Trinity Street, Chester, to rescue five screaming children and two adults. He suffered burns in the rescue. His heroism was rewarded with two further medals from life saving societies.

'Jim' Cleaver, a popular local bobby, retired in 1953 with the rank of Inspector after thirty years' service.

World War II Drama

On the night of 14th August, 1940, Detective Sergeant 'Jim' Cleaver was returning in his car to the police station with a burglar named Jones. Suddenly, they spotted a Heinkel bomber with smoke pouring from its tail, hotly pursued by two Spitfires. The plane crashed in Bumpers Lane. Together, policeman and burglar, rushed to the scene and 'arrested' five members of the Luftwaffe's crack Condor Squadron. For the Germans, it meant a prisoner of war camp: for Jones, the story ended happily. His case was suspended *sine-die* and he joined the Army!

Professor Robert Newstead MSc. FRS JP

Primarily an entomologist, he was, for over fifty years, Chester's leading archæologist, especially remembered for his excavations of the Roman Amphitheatre and as the first Curator of the Grosvenor Museum. What began as a hobby developed into a passion and the Newstead Gallery, displaying Roman Chester and many of his 'finds', is a worthy memorial. Internationally recognised, he received the freedom of the City in 1936. He is buried in Overleigh Cemetery.

PHOTO—THE CHESTER ARCHAEOLOGICAL SOCIETY

ROBERT NEWSTEAD (1859—1947)

◄ IN 1905/06 ROBERT NEWSTEAD WAS LIVING AT NO 65 (WITCOMBE VILLA) AND IN 1917/18 AT NO 67 (ST MARY'S COTTAGE), BOTH BUILT FOR THE FIRST DUKE OF WESTMINSTER AND ATTRIBUTED TO JOHN DOUGLAS (1830—1911) (EDWARD HUBBARD: 'THE WORK OF JOHN DOUGLAS' — THE VICTORIAN SOCIETY 1911 CATALOGUE OF WORKS P 239)

PHOTO—LEN MORGAN

Geoff Reynolds lived in Appleyards Lane and attended St Mary's C of E School in Handbridge and, later, the City Grammar School. He was a teacher at Overleigh School from 1959 to 1993.

His services included:

49 years with the Cheshire Schools FA and with the Chester Schools FA
(Hon Sec 1963—to date)
English Schools FA Council (1985—93)

MARGARET PHILLIPS

PHOTO—WENDY MOORCROFT

GEOFF REYNOLDS

PHOTO—COURTESY OF GEOFF REYNOLDS

▲ GEOFF REYNOLDS RECEIVING HIS MBE FROM HER MAJESTY QUEEN ELIZABETH AT BUCKINGHAM PALACE ON 10TH MAY 2000 FOR 'SERVICES TO THE COMMUNITY'

◄ NURSE MARGARET PHILLIPS (MIDWIFE) OF 4, HUGH STREET WITH ONE OF HER 'DELIVERIES' IN 1933. NOTE THE BAG ON HER BIKE 'IN WHICH THE BABIES CAME'!
THE PHOTOGRAPH WAS TAKEN IN 1934/35 ON THE CORNER OF HARTINGTON STREET AND ECCLESTON AVENUE OPPOSITE THE GREEN

Nurse Annie Ellis

Some will remember Nurse Annie Ellis, certified midwife, of 6 Belgrave Place, who married one of the Hanmers from Old Wrexham Road and moved to Ebury Place.

PAT POPE

PHOTO—COURTESY OF PAT POPE

▲ PAT ON DUTY IN CUPPIN STREET BEFORE SHE MOVED TO EATON ROAD c1967, DUE TO THE CLOSURE OF ST FRANCIS' JUNIOR SCHOOL

MRS PAT POPE AT BUCKINGHAM PALACE, 25TH NOVEMBER 1997, ▶ HAVING RECEIVED HER MBE FOR 'SERVICES TO THE COMMUNITY'

PHOTO—COURTESY OF PAT POPE

ALDERMAN LEONARD EDWARDS

PHOTO—MARTIN MERIDITH

ALDERMAN LEONARD EDWARDS ON HIS RETIREMENT, CONFRONTED BY A CROWD OF WELL-WISHERS OUTSIDE HIS CHEMIST SHOP IN QUEEN'S PARK VIEW ON 15TH APRIL 1978. THE MAYOR OF CHESTER, SHEILA GARSTON, PRESENTED HIM WITH A SILVER SALVER (AND A BOUQUET OF FLOWERS FOR MRS EDWARDS) FOR FORTY YEARS' SERVICE TO THE COMMUNITY. ▼

▲ LEN AND RUTH EDWARDS.
LEN WAS MAYOR IN 1971. HE WAS ELECTED A CITY COUNCILLOR ON 24TH MAY 1961 AND RETIRED ON 15TH APRIL 1978. MRS EDWARDS (NÉE WILLIAMS) WAS A FORMER PUPIL OF THE CITY HIGH SCHOOL FOR GIRLS.

PHOTO—CHESTER OBSERVER

MARGARET ANN BYATT – LORD MAYOR AND ADMIRAL OF THE DEE 1993/4

PHOTO—COURTESY OF MARGARET BYATT

PHOTO—QUEEN'S PARK HIGH SCHOOL

▲ WITH ANDREW FIRMAN (HEAD) AND PETER BYATT AT THE HANDBRIDGE COMMUNITY PLAY, 'ACROSS THE RIVER', QUEEN'S PARK HIGH SCHOOL 19TH APRIL 1993

◄ MARGARET ANN BYATT, 7 EASTERN PATHWAY, QUEEN'S PARK, INSTALLED AS LORD MAYOR OF CHESTER IN MAY 1993 WITH HER CONSORT, PETER. DURING HER TERM OF OFFICE, SHE ATTENDED SOME 850 FUNCTIONS! 'IT WAS AN HONOUR TO HAVE REPRESENTED THE PEOPLE OF THE HANDBRIDGE AREA AS ONE OF THEIR CITY COUNCILLORS FOR 16 YEARS'.
L TO R: NEW SHERIFF LIZ BOLTON; DEPUTY LADY MAYORESS BARBARA SMITH; DEPUTY LORD MAYOR CLLR GORDON SMITH; LORD MAYOR'S CONSORT PETER BYATT

ALDERMAN BERT REYNOLDS OBE

Sheriff of Chester (1942) Bert Reynolds lived at 6 Meadows Lane, Handbridge, and was an auditor with LMS Railways. He served for many years on the National Executive of the Railway Clerks Association.

F C HIGNETT

+ *Frederick Chrystie Hignett of 5, St John's Road, Queen's Park died on 21st December 1996 aged 85; beloved husband of Mary and father of Brian. Funeral Service at St Mary's Parish Church at 12:30 on 4th January 1997.*
Chester Chronicle
27th December 1996

He was a former Mayor of Chester (1975) and largely responsible for the provision of the Northgate Arena. +

PHOTO—JOAN DE WINTON (DAUGHTER)

INSTALLED AS MAYOR IN 1948 WITH LEFT TO RIGHT: ALDERMEN CHARLES SCONCE, KATE CLARKE AND ROBERT MATTHEWSON
BERT REYNOLD WAS AWARDED AN OBE (1949) FOR SERVICES TO THE COMMUNITY

LIONEL THOMAS CASWELL ROLT

PHOTO—LEN MORGAN

ROLT'S BIRTHPLACE, 7 SOUTH VIEW VILLAS, EATON ROAD, HANDBRIDGE – *'IN 1910 THE RESPECTABLE OUTER SUBURBAN FRINGE OF THE CITY, POISED BETWEEN THE EXTREMES OF WEALTH AND POVERTY.'*
ROLT'S AUTOBIOGRAPHY

PHOTO—LONGMANS

ROLT WITH HIS 'NEW TOY' IN 1933 – A 1903 HUMBER

L T C Rolt—Engineer (1910—1974)

He is world famous for his work with canals and boats. Ellesmere Port Boat Museum, with the world's largest collection of canal craft, has a gallery named after him. A visit as a youngster to the narrow gauge railway at Eaton Hall inspired his career as an engineer. He formed the Inland Waterways Association to preserve canals and boats for leisure enjoyment (eg Llangollen Canal). He was the author of a number of books, including his autobiography, 'Landscape with Machines' (Longmans 1971).

MARGARET FARRA

PHOTO—COURTESY OF MARGARET FARRA

PHOTO—LEN MORGAN

▲ QUEEN'S SCHOOL, CHESTER, FOUNDED IN 1878

Margaret Farra, Headmistress of Queen's School (1973—1989)

Born in York and a graduate (MSc) of Bedford College, London, Miss Farra was the headmistress of Plymouth High School for Girls for six years. She was then appointed Headmistress of Queen's School, Chester, in 1973 and retired in 1989. She has lived in Queen's Park for over thirty years.

During Miss Farra's headship, Queen's School reverted to its original independent status (1975), saw the inauguration of the Parents' Association (1974) and the establishment of a bursary scheme (1979) for girls needing financial assistance. The School gained a high reputation for academic achievement, with strong musical and sporting traditions, encouraged by a dedicated and energetic staff.

MRS ANNIE YATES

PHOTO—SUE BELL

▲ ANNIE YATES PRESENTED WITH A BASKET OF FLOWERS BY THE DUCHESS OF WESTMINSTER ON THE OCCASION OF HER 100TH BIRTHDAY

Mrs Annie Yates of Belgrave Place lived to see her 100th birthday and to receive the customary congratulations from the Queen in 1994. In the photograph, she is seen receiving a basket of flowers from the Duchess of Westminster at her birthday party at the Community Centre in Queen's Park High School. The voluntary day centre cares for a dozen frail and elderly members of the Handbridge area with the help of a social worker and Cheshire County Council. A management committee, whose chairman from 1991 to 1993 was Peter Byatt, is now in the capable and devoted hands of Sue Bell and a team of volunteers.

From School to College

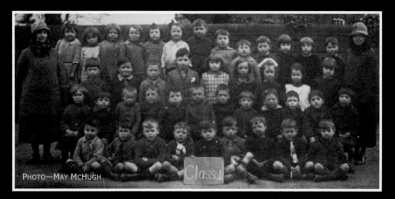

St Mary's C of E School Handbridge: Class of 1925

PHOTO—MAY MCHUGH

EDUCATION ACTS

1870 Education - free and compulsory for 5—12 year olds

1902 Local Education Authorities created to be responsible for education including 12+

1944 Education in 3 stages – Primary (5-11), Secondary (11—15+) and Further: leaving age – 15

St Mary's C E School

THE FORMER ST MARY'S
C OF E SCHOOL ▶
PHOTO—LEN MORGAN

St Mary's Key Dates

(CRO/Z/DES/10)

1860 St Mary's Infant School built.

1876 Enlarged for girls.

1886 School extended with the generous help of the first Duke of Westminster.

1887 Boys' department added.

1900 Mrs Froggatt appointed Headmistress (1900 – 1930).

1902 Enlargements to school and playground.

1911 25th May: School closes for Coronation week.

1930 Miss Eileen Bancroft appointed Headmistress (1930 – 1956) Roll 196.

1935 Holiday for George V's Silver Jubilee.

1942 School Inspection – 'Tone of school, excellent.' Roll 120; attended, 59; 33 cases of measles and scarlet fever.

1946 1st June: Victory Celebration party.

PHOTO—MAY McHUGH

LIFE IN SCHOOL AT THE START OF THE CENTURY. ST MARY'S IN c1900.
NOTE THAT MOST OF THE GIRLS HAVE DOLLS WITH THEM IN THE CLASS.

DORIS GREATBANKS (GILLIAN'S MOTHER) IS 2ND ROW DOWN, 3RD CHILD FROM RIGHT.

MRS EMILY ROBERTS (NÉE EDWARDS) (TEACHER, FAR RIGHT) WAS A FORMER PUPIL. IT WAS VERY UNUSUAL FOR A MARRIED WOMAN TO BE A TEACHER IN THOSE DAYS.

2ND ROW DOWN, 4TH FROM LEFT IS DOROTHY WILD, HERBERT'S SISTER (SEE P 32).

BOTTOM ROW, 2ND LEFT IS BERTHA TOTTY, WHO MARRIED TREVOR WALTERS (SEE P 64), A PROFESSIONAL FOOTBALLER FROM GREENWAY STREET. ▶

PHOTO—GILLIAN BROWN

▲ STANDARD 4, 1924

PHOTO—BOB JONES

◀ 1952

1948 St Mary's became a Primary School for 5 - 11 year olds.

1952 HMI Inspection. On roll, 115. "This is a good school under a kind and industrious head of 20 years' service, supported by a conscientious staff of 3 assistants."

1972 St Mary's became a First School under a new head, Mrs C A Baldwin. (See over)

1984 St Mary's First School closed. Children moved to Overleigh Primary School (ages 5 – 11)

1984 – 1998 St Andrew's Special Education Unit, Head, Mrs P S Sanderson occupied the premises.

St Andrew's Special Education Unit

HANDBRIDGE PRIMARY SCHOOL FOOTBALL TEAM 1948 ▲

BACK   JOHN LIVERSAGE, ALAN HUGHES, TOMMY MOORCROFT
MIDDLE TERRY PRICE, KENNY THOMPSON, BARRIE HIPKISS
FRONT   PETER ROWLANDSON, CECIL MEACOCK, BILLY WILLETS
        KENNY HODKINSON BERNARD PRICE

PHOTO—CHESTER CHRONICLE

PRESENTED BY
Y CLUB OF GREAT BRITAI
NCHESTER COMMITTEE

MRS P SANDERSON & DISTRICT EDUCATION OFFICER, NOEL ST JOHN WILLIAMS

THE VARIETY CLUB OF GREAT BRITAIN PRESENTS A MINI-BUS TO ST ANDREW'S SPECIAL EDUCATION UNIT

Handbridge First and Middle Schools 1972–84

1965 LEAs compelled to submit plans to abolish the 11-plus examination for the selection of pupils for secondary education.

1972 Cheshire County Council favoured comprehensive secondary schools for all. Chester LEA chose First Schools (pupils 5 – 8), Middle Schools (pupils 8 – 12) and High Schools (pupils 12 – 16).

1980 Education Act gave parents the right to express a preference for child's school.

1982 LEA organised courses for Governing Bodies (including parent and teacher representatives).

Handbridge St Mary's C E Controlled First School (Pupils 5 – 8)

4 Sep 1972 School opened with 281 pupils; 8 classes, 50 – 60+ in each age group. Headmistress, Miss C A Baldwin (1972 – 84); Deputy, Mrs M C McAllen (1972 – 84). Falling birth rate nationally (St Mary's 1975 [230] - 1982 [130]) led to class and school closures as uneconomic.

22 Jun 1982 Decision to close First School: pupils to transfer to Overleigh Primary School.

Overleigh Middle School (Pupils 8– 12)

Heads Mr Frank Dutton (1972 – 76); Mr Peter Maskery (1976 – 84). School took over St Bede's Secondary RC School Buildings.

1984 Middle School ceased and First School incorporated to become…
Overleigh St Mary's C E Primary School (Pupils 5 – 11).

OVERLEIGH MIDDLE SCHOOL STAFF 1980

PHOTO — COURTESY OF G.M REYNOLDS

BACK ENID SHAW, BRENDA JAMES, DOT WILLIAMS, PAT FLETCHER, LIZ JONES, SHEILA TOMLINSON, VAL CLEEVES.
MIDDLE KAREN EASTON, VAL HOLROYD, GEOFF REYNOLDS, STEVE KINDRED, DAVE WATSON, PAT HODDER, SHIRLEY BROWN, SANDRA JONES.
FRONT JAN SPRATLEY, SHEILA GEORGE, PETER MASKERY, MARION GRIFFIN, ANN BELL, CAROL VRLEC

ROLF MEETS STAGE-STRUCK PUPILS

Stagestruck pupils at Overleigh Middle School had some exciting visitors, when Rolf Harris and 70 members of staff from the BBC came to record "Rolf at Christmas" 1980. The 35 minute show featured 175 boys and girls (aged 8 to 11) singing four songs; 'Santa Claus medley', 'Christmas Card medley', 'Little Donkey' and 'Six White Bloomers'.

The producer of the show, James Moir, said that Chester was chosen because of its historic connections and because it had not been featured before in such a programme.

Rolf commented: 'We have had super co-operation from the children, who I think, have been the best ever musically.'

Mr Noel St John Williams, the district education officer, said: 'Overleigh was chosen because it met the BBC's requirements: staging facilities; hall; parking etc.' Catering and technical help were provided by QPHS.

PHOTO—NOEL ST JOHN WILLIAMS

ROLF HARRIS' CHRISTMAS SHOW 1980 ▲▼

SPECIAL CLASS VISITS ST MARY'S CHURCH

PHOTO—COURTESY OF PETER MASKERY

ROLF WITH JOANNE AND JONATHAN MASKERY▲

FRANK DUTTON AND STAFF, 1975—76

PHOTO — VALERIE CLEEVES

BACK   GM REYNOLDS; G LLOYD; MISS P FLETCHER; MRS S ADAMS; MRS J SPRATLEY; MRS V HOLROYD; MRS P MADDEN; MRS MOODY; S JONES; S BARNET

FRONT   MRS J HUNTER; MRS B YOUNG; MRS J DAVIES; MISS L GREEN; F DUTTON (HEAD); R EVANS; MISS P HILL; MRS O GOFF; MRS V CLEEVES

Overleigh St Mary's C E Primary School 1984 – to date

Head:
Mr Peter Maskery 1984 – 2004

PHOTO I BIRCHENOUGH

▲ THE SCHOOL BUILDINGS – THE SCHOOL HALL (FORMERLY ST BEDE'S SECONDARY SCHOOL)

School Awards / Achievements

Academic Achievement: Beacon School; Gold Sports mark, Gold Artsmark for music, drama and visual arts.

Partnership school undertaking training of teachers.

HM Conference hosted at school; Visit of Israeli Minister of Education

To Noel with many happy memories Peter.

Overleigh St Mary's invites you to a
farewell celebration on the retirement of

Peter Maskery

Monday March 29th
7.30 to 9.00 pm

at Overleigh St Mary's School Hall

RSVP to the School Office by March 18th

▲ RETIREMENT INVITATION TO NOEL ST JOHN WILLIAMS, WHO AS DISTRICT EDUCATION OFFICER APPOINTED PETER MASKERY 27 YEARS BEFORE.

PHOTO—PETER MASKERY

▲ MR MASKERY, THE HEAD AT OVERLEIGH SCHOOLS FOR OVER 27 YEARS, WITH A GROUP OF CHILDREN AND THEIR MODELS 'TRANSPORT IN THE FUTURE'

▲ OVERLEIGH ST MARY'S NATIVITY PLAY DECEMBER 1991

THE SCHOOL SUPPORTS MANY CHARITIES
AND COMMUNITY PROJECTS.

▼ SCHOOL PRODUCTION 2003 – "OLIVER"

SCHOOL ORCHESTRA 1996 ▲
CENTRE, KATIE JONES (LEN'S GRAND-DAUGHTER).

MR GLEDHILL'S CLASS 1996 ▼

A Specialist Science College
Committed to providing the best Catholic education for all.

Headteachers:

St Bede's

Mr Bernard Dowd	1953 – 67
Mr Michael Balfe	1967 – 72

Catholic High School

Mr Michael Balfe	1972 – 89
Miss C McCann	1989 – 93
Mrs V Ratchford	1993– 2003

MR MICHAEL BALFE ▼   ▼ MISS C McCANN

◀ CANON FRANCIS MURPHY VF
CHAIRMAN OF GOVERNORS
ST BEDE'S   1959—72
CATHOLIC HS 1972—78

PARISH PRIEST 1959—82
DIED   1990

MR BERNARD DOWD (HEAD) & MISS A C DOUGLAS (DEPUTY HEAD)
ST BEDE'S RC SECONDARY SCHOOL
FAR UPPER LEFT – OVER THE DOORS SHOWN ABOVE, RELIEF OF ST BEDE

History

1953 St Bede's R C Secondary School opened (now Overleigh St Mary's C E Primary School buildings).

1972 Renamed Catholic High School (moved to present location: buildings previously occupied by Overleigh Secondary Modern School).

2002 Awarded Special Science College status. £50 000 raised in support

GIRLS' SUMMER SCHOOL UNIFORM 1972 ▶

GREEN CHECK DRESS;

MOSS GREEN BLAZER WITH SCHOOL BADGE;

OPTIONAL BROWN FLAT-HEELED SANDALS.

(STILL USED TODAY)

JULIA MURRAY, WHO MODELLED THE UNIFORM IN THE SCHOOL BROCHURE, IS NOW JULIA LEONARD AND HAS 3 CHILDREN PRESENTLY ATTENDING THE SCHOOL. SHE WAS A SECRETARY IN THE SCHOOL OFFICE.

PHOTO – CATHOLIC HIGH SCHOOL

L TO R: ALEXANDRA McCANN; LEE BENNION; NATHAN BECKETT; MARY (?); RT REV BISHOP GRAY; MISS C McCANN; MARK BLUNDELL; MICHAEL PEARSON; PAUL CADDEN; STEPHEN PAYNE.

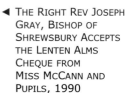

◀ THE RIGHT REV JOSEPH GRAY, BISHOP OF SHREWSBURY ACCEPTS THE LENTEN ALMS CHEQUE FROM MISS McCANN AND PUPILS, 1990

Pupils participate in a wide range of activities, including sponsored events for charities and national appeals. The School was awarded Specialist Science College status in 2002 with pupils, staff, parents and local business groups raising £50,000.

In 1989, the School Soccer XI won the English Schools Nabisco Trophy and the Cheshire County Schools FA Shield.

▲ EXCHANGE VISIT TO NORMANDY 2000

MRS V RATCHFORD INTERVIEWED BY 6TH FORM PUPILS
'THE HEAD WANTED TO BE A PROFESSIONAL HORSE RIDER BUT
ENDED UP TEACHING!'

SCHOOL MUSICAL PRODUCTION OF ▶
"GUYS AND DOLLS"

▼ FENCING

POSSENT QUIA
POSSE VIDENTUR

Chester City High School for Girls 1905 – 1970

Headmistresses:

Miss C J M Hubback   (1905 – 09)

Miss H M Footman   (1909 – 34)

Miss N Richards   (1935 – 59)

Miss Dorothy Preston (1959 – 70)

PHOTO—IAN BIRCHENOUGH

THE IMPRESSIVE FRONTAGE OF THE ▶
CITY HIGH SCHOOL FOR GIRLS, QUEEN'S PARK
BUILT 1909 – 12
BY W T LOCKWOOD, SON OF THOMAS M LOCKWOOD

History

23 Jan 1905 Miss Hubback (Head), 2 assistants and 37 girls assembled at The Pavilion, the Race Course, to found The City and County School for Girls.

15 Jan 1909 First meeting of Old Girls' Association. Annual Subscription, 6d.

25 May 1912 150 girls moved to Queen's Park , Handbridge. '*As we moved out of our school on the Race Course, the horses moved in.*' Agnes Rahill, pupil.

1941 Chester City High School moved into its own building (City Grammar School for Boys moves next door).

Jul 1971 School ceased to exist as a separate entity

There is a <u>need in the City for a girls' school</u> similar in type to the boys' school at the Museum. Such a school would be very successful and would not compete with the Queen's School. Provision for <u>about 250 girls</u> might be made in the same block as the proposed new boys' school but the school should be conducted as a separate school.

A Dufton HMI for Secondary Education
9th May 1904

(<u>Recommended at the same time</u>: 'The Day School for Boys at the Grosvenor Museum should have a new building for 250 boys.')

<u>Subjects of Instruction</u>: 'a good grounding in the three Rs, a modern language or two in the spoken form… Scientific teaching from about the 12th year, together with a good mathematical instruction, domestic economy – <u>a real preparation for the world's work'.</u>

Fees: 4½ guineas per annum, including text books and stationery.

County Record Office /Z/DES/37

1925 HANDICRAFT CLASS ▼

PHOTO — HC YI/5/76

Service of Thanksgiving

COMMEMORATING

THE 50TH ANNIVERSARY
OF THE
FOUNDING OF THE SCHOOL

CHESTER CATHEDRAL

WEDNESDAY, 26TH JANUARY, 1955
AT 6-0 P.M.

On Saturday, a dinner will be held at the Blossoms Hotel, at which
it is hoped the first Headmistress, Miss Hubbock, will be present.

How did we get to school? Not by special bus but by train from all parts in the town, as far as Bridge Street. Hoole girls joined the trek of train girls (from Birkenhead, Helsby, Frodsham and Ellesmere Port) down City Road, through Grosvenor Park, along the Groves, over the Old Dee Bridge, through the slums of Handbridge (deep alleys and entries like the 'Courts' of Lower Bridge Street) to the school.

It would have been quicker to come over the narrow swing bridge which spanned the Dee (the Suspension Bridge) and through Queen's Park – but that would have led us past the Boys' entrance, and given us too much opportunity for fun and games! (see right)

No cars ever fetched or carried us from school. Girls coming in from Pulford (now served by about four buses an hour) had to cycle. Mary Crowe, who came from Home Farm on the Duke's estate, came by pony and trap. No member of staff owned a car. The headmistress, Miss Footman, bought her first car in the late 1920s and proudly took her class to the front door to see it.

Who were we? The daughters of butchers, bakers, candle-stick makers etc. More than half were fee-paying. There was a great competition for entrants: tests were set and marked by the Headmistress and Staff. The library (a little room under the eaves) was also the Lower and Upper VI form rooms, and was used by the 'cold dinner' girls. No gym or art room nor such refinements as geography, music or MO's rooms. No uniforms save large 'boaters' with the daisy badge on a woollen cap (any colour) in winter.

Agnes Rahill Reminiscences, *The Inkwell*
CRO/Z/DES/38

PHOTO—CRO/Z/DES/38

A GRAMMAR SCHOOL PREFECT ON DUTY AT THE BRIDGE 1961

HOCKEY XI 1931-32
LIVERPOOL & DISTRICT SECONDARY SCHOOLS' CHAMPIONS

PHOTO—CRO/Z/DES/38/21

BACK: M TEASDILL; E SMITH; E LARGE; N COTTRILL; M HUGHES; D BOOKER
FRONT: M GRIFFITHS; M PRITCHARD; A BRACEGIRDLE; M WILDING; P LEACH

PHOTO — CRO/Z/DES/38

THE JOINT CAST OF 'MARIA MARTIN', A VICTORIAN MELODRAMA- 1966
SALLY ANCLIFF (MARIA); PAMELA FARRINGTON (DAME MARTIN); FJ IVES (SUFFOLK RUSTIC);
S ADAMS (WILLIAM CORDER); RUTH BENDER (ANNE)

City Grammar School for Boys 1902 – 1970

Headmasters:

Mr J Wilkins	(1912 – 37)	Mr J Challacombe	(1942 – 48)
Mr E Ayres	(1938 – 42)	Mr C Race	(1948 – 70)

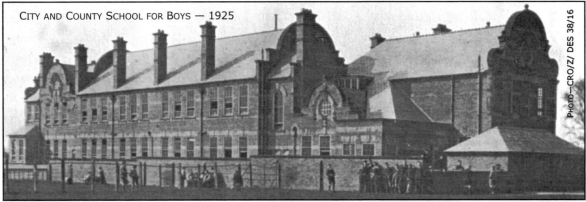

CITY AND COUNTY SCHOOL FOR BOYS — 1925

PHOTO—CRO/Z/ DES 38/16

History

1892 Technical Day School opened in the Grosvenor Museum with 21 pupils.

1902 Technical Day School became a secondary school.

1907 Name changed to 'City and County School for Boys'.

1912 School moved to new buildings in Queen's Park.

1938 Name changed to 'Chester City Grammar School for Boys'.

1939 New Wing added.

1941 Moved into new premises in Queen's Park built by Charles Greenwood.

1971 On the re-structuring of education in Chester, the school became part, along with the adjacent City High School and the nearby Overleigh Secondary Modern School, of the new Queen's Park Comprehensive School.

PHOTO—CRO/Z/DES/38   PHOTO—CRO/Z/DES/38   PHOTO—CRO/Z/DES/38

J WILKINS   J CHALLACOMBE CBE   C RACE

PHOTO—CRO/Z/DES/30

SCHOOL JUN XI 1930 / 31

BACK   MR BROOMFIELD (GROUNDSMAN), S GANDY, W N HIGGINS, M W EARLAM,
M E GREGORY, F W POUNTNEY, J L RICHARDSON.
FRONT J I MITCHELL, W H FODEN, J A MOORE (CAPTN), MR R H RAMSHAW, E VENABLES, J N CRAINE.
 S JOHNSON,   J L CHARLTON

MR ERNEST BROMFIELD – 52, ALLINGTON PLACE, HANDBRIDGE WAS A PROFESSIONAL FOOTBALLER (STOCKPORT COUNTY) AND CRICKETER (DENABY CC) BEFORE BECOMING GROUNDSMAN AND COACH FOR THE CITY GRAMMAR SCHOOL.

School Song (tune—Haydn Emperor theme)

Deva Deva gaudeamus

Fave tu cannentibus

Dulce flumen, Te canamus

Fave tu cannentibus

Dulce flumen, Te canamus

Fave tu cannentibus

Deva, O Deva, let us rejoice

Favour us with your music

Softly (flowing) River, we praise you in song

1939 –1945
WAR MEMORIAL

Anwyl J	(1921/26)	Lawrence G	(1934/39)
Astbury T E	(1935/40)	Lawrence W G	(1927/32)
Bewley T L		Ledsham R	(1933/38)
Biggs W	(1932/37)	Lyne D H	(1931/36)
Brown D	(1933/38)	Marr W H	(1929/34)
Carr E J	(1924/30)	Matthews C H	(1934/49)
Chambers R F	(1924/29)	Mealing W D	(1935/39)
Chaplin K	(1923/26)	Melia J L	(1934/40)
Comyn J		Poole K S	(1931/38)
Davies D		Price R F	(1931/36)
Davies N C	(1925/29)	Rosbottom J H	(1925/30)
Disbury G F	(1933/40)	Rowe H C	(1930/34)
Diskuy G F		Smith J R	(1920/24)
Dobinson W B	(1934/39)	Spencer J A	
Donovan J G	(1932/37)	Tatnall J B	(1918/23)
Evans J G	(1933/38)	Vickers D T	
Formstone S C	(1932/37)	Waters T W	(1927/32)
Gordon J A	(1933/41)	Weaver B F	(1933/38)
Hamilton A M	(1935/39)	Whitley H	(1933/37)
Hazelhurst G T E	(1929/35)	Whitley J W	
Hobson B F	(1930/35)	Williams J R S	(1933/38)
Hollis T F	(1934/39)	Wood T	(1930/38)
Hooper R	(1938/40)	Woodcock N	
Hughes H	(1929/34)		

Peace Returns to the School – April 1946

I am glad to write for the first peace-time edition of 'The Inkwell' after the difficulties of war time publication – one of the signs that normal conditions are creeping back! An even more welcome sign is the return of all those members of the staff who served in the Forces. Only a few months ago, they were scattered all over the world—Freddy Matthews (War Office, served in both World Wars); Johnny Stell (France and Germany); Mr Morris (3 years' captivity in Singapore); Les Harris (India). The School will be the richer for their experience and the stronger for their presence.

The 1944 Education Act has created a new system of national education. The chief changes for our school have been the abolition of fees and the establishment of the Technical Course. The new annexe will provide the necessary Workshops and Laboratory (including a Language laboratory), its outer ugliness balanced by its inner usefulness. Our pioneering experiment of blending two types of secondary education, Grammar and Technical, in one school is being watched with interest by parents and educationalists.

J. Challacombe

They also left their footprints in the sand of time.

P K Byatt (French)	1952/71
J Druery (Physics)	1919/48
F H Fraser (Woodwork)	1927/57
J W Green (Art)	1907 – 28
R H Ramshaw (History)	1921/58
J Stell (Art)	25 years
J W Marriott (Handicrafts)	1892/1927
F M Matthews (English, French)	1923/51
W E Morgan (English, History)	1913/50
R C Penfold MC JP (French)	1920/55

THE STAFF 1930 / 31   CREDIT

BACK   S. CAPPER, W J BRADNOCK, B A LEWIS, F H FRASER, C G HAWKINS,
R C PENFOLD, G W C SALVESEN, J DRUERY.
FRONT H W LAWSON, F MATTHEWS, W E MORGAN, J K WILKINS (HEAD), T ROBERTS,
R H RAMSHAW, T JACQUES.

◄ THE *INKWELL* WAS FIRST PUBLISHED IN NOVEMBER 1923

MEMBERS OF THE 1948 ► ROWING CLUB USING THE FACILITIES OF THE CHESTER ROWING CLUB. THE SCHOOL BUILT ITS OWN FACILITY NEAR THE MEADOWS IN THE 1960s.

Overleigh Secondary Modern School 1953 – 1970

OVERLEIGH ▶
SECONDARY MODERN
SCHOOL.
SINCE 1970, THE
BUILDING HAS BEEN
OCCUPIED BY THE
CATHOLIC HIGH
SCHOOL

PHOTO—LEN MORGAN

Headmasters:

Mr J T Hutcheson   1954 – 1963
Mr John Scott   1963 – 1970

History

1953   Love Street School (1909 –1967) became a Secondary Modern School for Girls. The boys transferred to Overleigh Secondary Modern in a new building in Handbridge costing £150,000, with 22 acres of land acquired from the Duke of Westminster. The school had a grammar stream.

1970   Following changes to comprehensive schools, the Overleigh pupils were transferred to Queen's Park High School. Its premises were occupied by St Bede's Roman Catholic Secondary Modern, later to become the Catholic High School.

School Record

In its short life, Overleigh developed an excellent record of academic achievement and extra−curricular activities with a dedicated staff and supportive parents.

'We were very proud of our school and its achievements,' said old boy, Councillor and Sheriff of Chester, Terry Ralph (see football photograph on opposite page, front row, end right).

BACK   L WALTERS; J ADAMS; N READING; E JONES; L WRIGHT
2ND ROW   J FALGATE; F DALLIMORE; J MAUGHAN; J DENNING; E ELLIS; D JONES; JOHN SMITH
3RD ROW   W TURNER; J POWELL; R WAINWRIGHT; JIM SMITH; A DONOVAN; H DREW; GM REYNOLDS; J RANK; G BOULTON; D HOLLINS
FRONT   J HOUGH; MA JONES; COE MORGAN; R ROBERTS; R ZANKER (ACTING HEAD); W JONES; R DUNLEY; D HARTLEY; J EVANS

PHOTO — COURTESY OF G M REYNOLDS   OVERLEIGH SECONDARY MODERN STAFF, 1963—64

Sport

A message from the Sports Editor of the Chester Chronicle:

Any school's team aspiring to sporting honours in Chester and District has to beat Overleigh – and the record books are full of those who failed!

Whether it be on the soccer field, the athletics track or in the swimming pool, Overleigh boys have been the mainstays of many a Chester schoolboys' side with some going on to greater rewards – Alan Tarbuck (Everton), Paul Hallows (Bolton), Brian Woodall and Graham Pugh (Sheffield Wednesday). Trevor Walters from Greenway Street played for Chester and Wales.

SOCCER TEAM 1962 – 63
TERRY RALPH (FRONT ROW, END RIGHT)

School Magazine 1964

OVERLEIGH

The Magazine
of
Overleigh Secondary School
Chester

No. 1   June. 1964

HEADMASTER JOHN SCOTT WITH HIS PREFECTS ▶
1964

The school choir competed in the International Music Eisteddfod at Llangollen and gave a number of concerts around Chester, including Handbridge Congregational Church and the Cathedral.

There were school camps in Abersoch and the Outer Hebrides and school visits to York, Liverpool (to see the Vienna Boys' Choir), London and Switzerland.

Parents and Old Boys raised the money for an 'Outdoor' swimming pool which resulted in many County swimming champions!

PHOTO—SCHOOL MAGAZINE

Overleigh's Epitaph 1970

In this year the country is celebrating the Centenary of the 1870 Education Act. In 1873 a Headmaster noted in his logbook 'forced to cane the student teacher for playing marbles with the older boys'.

Chester is about to adopt a Comprehensive School system. This will mean the death of Overleigh Secondary Modern School and the scattering of its staff to the four winds. The corridors will echo in future to the patter of tiny feet. For a school with such a wonderful record and such first class facilities, the change will only be regretted.

John Booth of Form 5G, 1970

Queen's Park High School 1970 – to date

An 11 - 18 Comprehensive School incorporating a specialist Visual Arts College
serving its young people and the local community.

Working together to promote excellence in learning and acheivement for all.

Headmasters:

Mr Ken Munden	1970 – 1989
Mr Andrew Firman	1989 – to date

MR K MUNDEN   MR A FIRMAN

History

1970 Amalgamation of City High School for Girls, City Grammar School for Boys, Overleigh Secondary Modern School for Boys to form Queen's Park High School.

1980 HMI Report: 'a good school with quality academic achievements and good examination results. There is a strict but caring atmosphere in the school with a dedicated and hard working staff under a thoughtful and knowledgeable leadership.'

1990 Education Industry Partnership Award.

1992 21st Anniversary Re-union attended by 700 former students and staff.

1996 HMI Report: '… a good and improving school.'

1997 Schools Curriculum Award (recognising work with the community).

1998 Extra Certificate of Distinction for out of school hours learning (clubs and activities).

1999 Sport England Sportsmark Award.

2001 Neil Fairbrother opened Indoor Cricket Centre of Excellence (£65,000 Lottery grant for Sports Hall).

2002 Visual Arts College status award. (Oct 2003 Gerald Scarfe official opening.)

2003 School Achievement Award

ALL DRESSED UP IN 1940'S GEAR FOR THE COMMUNITY PLAY
"ACROSS THE RIVER"
PERFORMED BY PUPILS AND LOCAL RESIDENTS

FROM LEFT TO RIGHT

YVONNE JONES NEE BELLIS	MARGARET GAULTON	CENTRE
PEARL EVANS	MONA EVANS	BETTY HUGHES
IRMA NEWTON	ANN COWARD	DORIS WILLCOCKS
MARGARET DAVIES	LEN MORGAN	HANNAH WILLIAMS (GIRL)

PHOTO—LEN MORGAN

Queen's Park High School presents

We Will Remember Them

85th Anniversary of the Battle of the Somme

Tuesday – Thursday 13th – 15th November, 2001

A presentation in Poetry, Music, Song and Drama

PHOTO — QPHS

▲HRH Princess Anne with Andrew Firman, Sue Bell (Chair of Governors), Karen Ward and Mark Sutton (6th Formers) at the presentation of the Schools Curriculum Award at the Barbican Theatre 1997

JOHN O'GROATS TO LAND'S END CHARITY RUN – 1983
WEST ROUTE TEAM ▼

PHOTO — QPHS

Sixteen boys and girls of all ages, plus sixteen members of staff, in 10 days and camping on the way, ran as a relay from John O'Groats to Land's End for charities. £23,000 was raised.
PATRON: His Grace, The Duke of Westminster.
Planned by Ken Munden and Edwina Bowers.

PHOTO — CHESTER & DISTRICT STANDARD 23 OCT 03

▲Gerald Scarfe, the well-known caricature artist opened the new specialist Visual Arts College, 21 Oct 2003
Rachel Welch presents Mr Scarfe with a piece of glass work
Rachel Welch, Gerald Scarfe, Tony Jackson (Arts College manager) and Simon Parker (Art Teacher)

PHOTO — QPHS

◄ Royal Society of British Artists Exhibition, 2003
Rosie Hawkins (Year 8HLN) with the President of the RSBA, Romeo Di Girolamo.
Rosie's work was displayed.

◄ Russ Abbot, TV performer, native of Hoole and former pupil of the City Grammar School, with Christine Robson and Yvonne Hughes at the Promises Auction, June 2000 in the Long Room, Eaton Hall.

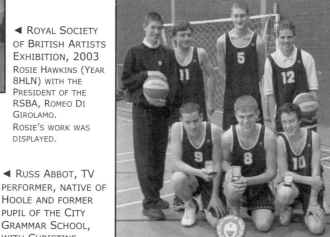

PHOTO — QPHS

▲The Year 10 Basketball Team won the Chester and District Championships in November, 2003
Liam Millington (Capt), James White, Gavin Walker, Chris Moore, Graham Cobden, Joe Batten and Daniel Taylor

PHOTO—WEST CHESHIRE COLLEGE

THE HANDBRIDGE CENTRE

Principals:

Mr Adrian Long	1963—1965
Mr L B Curzon	1965—1966
Mr Adrian Bristow	1966—1981
Mr C D Rees	1981—1993
Mr Neil Davies	1993—1995 (acting)
Mr R Munroe	1995—1999
Mrs Sarah Mogel	1999—to date

Centres:

Handbridge and Greenbank

Grange (Ellesmere Port)

Capenhurst (Technology)

History

1886 School of Art opened in the Grosvenor Museum.

1892 Technical Day School opened in Grosvenor Museum.

1912 Technical Day School moved to Queen's Park.

1956 College of FE built in Handbridge (School of Art became a department).

1963 Official opening of Chester College of Further Education by Lord Derby.

1983 Catering Courses began at Greenbank, Eaton Road.

1985 School of Art moved to Blacon.

1986 College re-named West Cheshire College.

PHOTO—ADRIAN BRISTOW

▲ MR ADRIAN BRISTOW

PHOTO—CHRIS REES

▲ MR CHRIS REES

COUNTY COUNCILLOR, J T HUMPHREYS, CHAIRMAN OF GOVERNORS, PRESENTING THE STUDENT OF THE YEAR AWARD IN 1975 IN THE PRESENCE OF MR ADRIAN BRISTOW (3RD ◀ LEFT) AND MEMBERS OF STAFF

PHOTO—ADRIAN BRISTOW

In 1998—9, the annual budget of £14.8 million provided for:

4 college centres and 8 adult education centres;

38 000 enrolments on 700 courses;

900 staff.

PRESENTATION BY THE PRINCIPAL, MRS SARA MOGEL, AND STUDENTS TO THE DUKE OF WESTMINSTER ▶

Activities and Courses— A wide range available from Academic to Vocational

PHOTO—WEST CHESHIRE COLLEGE

▲ MOTOR VEHICLE TECHNOLOGY.
LABORATORY AND ASSOCIATED ACTIVITIES ▼

Cours D'Été D'Anglais

POURQUOI VENIR À CHESTER?

- professeurs expérimentés et bien qualifiés
- ambience amicale
- laboratoire de langues
- bibliothèque bien equipée
- groupes multinationaux
- tous niveaux de langue anglaise
- collège public avec étudiants britanniques
- frais concurrentiels
- crèche pour les enfants
- ville historique avec des attractions du vingtième siècle

Nous attendons avec impatience le plaisir de vous accueillir à West Cheshire College

▲ LANGUAGE SUMMER SCHOOLS—1998

PERFORMING ARTS — (DRAMA AND DANCE) ▲

INFORMATION TECHNOLOGY 1991 ▼

▲ HAIRDRESSING AND BEAUTY THERAPY ▼

Greenbank Catering Centre

STUDENTS BEING TRAINED AT GREENBANK (R). LUNCH 1998. ▲
L TO R VILMA HOLMES; STUDENT; ANTONIA KAY

IN 1997 THE CHESTER AMNESTY INTERNATIONAL GROUP
CELEBRATED ITS 20 ANNIVERSARY WITH A VIETNAMESE FEAST,
PREPARED BY CATERING STUDENTS ▶

The Churches

PHOTO—DAVID BALDWIN

ST MARY'S SCHOOL (LEFT) AND CHURCH 1957

ST MARY WITHOUT-THE-WALLS
CONGREGATIONAL / UNITED REFORMED CHURCH
ST BARBARA'S GREEK ORTHODOX CHURCH
ST FRANCIS' AND ST WERBURGH'S RC CHURCHES

St Mary's without-the-walls

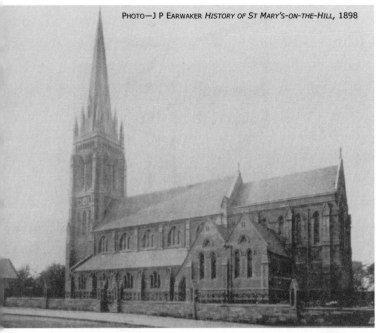

ST MARY'S CHURCH SHORTLY AFTER ITS CONSECRATION IN 1887 ▲

Rectors:

Henry Grantham	1885 – 1922
Andrew B Richie	1922 – 1925
Arthur W Sarson	1925 – 1949
Wyndham N D Thomas	1949 – 1965
Winston G Hurlow	1965 – 1983
Christopher W J Samuels	1983 – to date

From a tablet in St Mary's Church

A MEMORIAL PLAQUE, TO BE FOUND AT THE BASE OF ONE OF THE PILLARS, COMMEMORATING THE LAYING OF THE FOUNDATION STONE (1885) AND THE CONSECRATION OF THE CHURCH (1887) ▼

PHOTO—IAN BIRCHENOUGH

History

The original 12th century Parish Church, St Mary's on-the-Hill, was situated beside Chester Castle, the residence of the Earls of Chester. Richard de Coton was instituted Rector in the reign of King John (1199 – 1216). The Church, rebuilt in the Middle Ages, once ranked in importance with the Abbey Church, now the Cathedral and the Collegiate Church of St John (now St John's Church). Today, it is St Mary's Centre, owned by Cheshire County Council.

In 1887 the ancient parishes of St Mary's and St Bridget's were restructured and the new parish of St Mary's without-the-walls created south of the river.

◄ THE FIRST RECTOR OF THE NEW CHURCH OF ST MARY'S WITHOUT-THE-WALLS WAS THE REV H GRANTHAM 1885 – 1922

PHOTO—J P EARWAKER

Memories

Golden Wedding Recollection

Fifty years ago (on 3rd August 1890), Mary Ann Davies and her younger sister, Martha, daughters of a local sawyer, were married at the same time at St Mary's Church by Rev H Grantham to two popular Handbridge boys, Richard Relish and Joseph Price.

Observer, 10th August 1940

The fisher folk and others marked the occasion by presenting the biggest salmon the Dee had yielded that holiday weekend. Mr and Mrs Relish of 37 Pyecroft Street and Mr and Mrs Price of Greenway Street recalled that memorable day on Sunday, when they celebrated their golden weddings.

They also remembered the 29 old cottages on the site of St Mary's being removed and the occupants being rehoused on a new site in the vicinity of the cemetery. Excavations revealed 'a common burying place for Roman Legionaries'.

PHOTO—CHESTER CHRONICLE

▲ THE REV CANON CHRIS SAMUELS AND HIS WIFE, SARAH.
HE WAS APPOINTED A QUEEN'S CHAPLAIN AND PRESENTED TO THE
QUEEN ON 16TH JULY 2002

PHOTO—IAN BIRCHENOUGH

▲ THE MEMORIAL TABLET TO HUGH LUPUS, 1ST DUKE OF
WESTMINSTER, GIVEN BY A GRATEFUL CONGREGATION IN
1902

Writing in the Parish Magazine, 1st January 1900, the first Rector, Rev H Grantham, began:—It is with mixed feelings of thankfulness and sorrow that I address you at the opening of the year 1900—sorrow that the [Boer] War has brought much mourning and anxiety over our land and mourning for our most generous benefactor, Hugh Lupus, Duke of Westminster. Many of you will remember the consecration of our Church on 18th June (Waterloo Day) 1887: the laying of the foundation stones of the Church and Rectory (the Church by the Duke and the Rectory by the Duchess) in 1885: and the cottage property of Handbridge fifteen years ago with its wretched courts and surroundings rebuilt to provide comfortable and good dwellings for our people.

▲ THE VISIBLE SYMBOL OF HANDBRIDGE AND THE CENTRE OF
ITS SOCIAL AND SPIRITUAL LIFE.
PICTURE FROM THE COVER OF THE PARISH MAGAZINE,
© PETER GASTON (FORMERLY OF HANDBRIDGE)

▲ FROM THE COVER OF THE PARISH MAGAZINE
JANUARY 1900

THE BREAD BOX (1608)
LOAVES OF BREAD WERE PLACED ON THE SHELF FOR THE WORKING POOR OF THE PARISH. THE BOX WAS ORIGINALLY IN ST BRIDGET'S, WHITE FRIARS (DEMOLISHED 1828), REPLACED BY A NEW ST BRIDGET'S (DEMOLISHED 1892). THE BOX WAS THEN REMOVED TO ST MARY'S ON-THE-HILL TO BE FINALLY PLACED IN ST MARY'S WITHOUT-THE-WALLS IN 1973.

▲ CENTENARY FLOWER FESTIVAL 1887—1987
DIRECTED BY ANN COX WITH THE HELP OF CHESTER FLOWER CLUB AND ST MARY'S FLOWER GUILD ▼

▲ THE MEMORIAL WINDOW DEPICTING THE HOLY FAMILY IS DEDICATED TO REV H GRANTHAM

St Mary's is the garrison church of the Chester Garrison, the Rector being its chaplain. The East window showing St George in full armour is a memorial to those who gave their lives in World War I. The brass plate opposite this window commemorates the fallen in World War II.

PHOTO—LIZA MOORE

▲ ST MARY'S FÊTE 1949

ST MARY'S FÊTE 1949 ►
18TH JUNE 1949—REVELS ON THE RECTORY LAWN
THE ANNUAL GARDEN FETE PRESIDED OVER BY THE RECTOR, THE
REV W N DIGBY THOMAS, AND THE SHERIFF, COUNCILLOR W R
WILLIAMS, WHO, AS A KING'S SCHOOLBOY, HAD BEEN
CONFIRMED AT ST MARY'S.

ROSE QUEEN: MISS SHEILA YVONNE JONES
TRAIN BEARERS: PAMELA HIPKISS, MAUREEN DALE,
                JOSEPHINE BOTTING, JEAN BARWISE
FLOWER GIRLS: SYLVIA FROST, BRIDGET OWENS
CROWN BEARER: MARTIN MEREDITH

PHOTO—MARTIN MEREDITH

On Wednesday 14th June 1950 Joan Vickers (16), of 76 Allington Place, carried on the Rose Queen tradition, when she opened the Fête in the crowded Rectory Gardens. Resplendent in white taffeta with a cloak of pale pink and green velvet, she welcomed, with the Rector, Rev. Digby Thomas, Lady Simpson, the wife of Lt. Gen. Sir Frank Simpson, GOC in C Western Command. The infants of St Mary's School, trained by Miss E Bancroft, danced The Maypole. The Junior School gave an exhibition of boxing and gymnastics.

Chester Chronicle

PHOTO—LIZA MOORE

▲ JOAN VICKERS, THE ROSE QUEEN AND HER RETINUE—JUNE 1950

MAYPOLE DANCING IN THE INSTITUTE GARDEN, IN THE RECTORY GARDEN, AND THE CROWNING OF THE MAY QUEEN IN THE PLAYGROUND OF ST MARY'S SCHOOL, ARE ACTIVITIES LONG ASSOCIATED WITH ST MARY'S CHURCH.
ST MARY'S FÊTE
◀ 1989 AND 1964 ▼

St Mary's Church Parade — Whit Sunday, 1926

THE PARADE ▶ PASSING PERCY ROAD ALONG QUEEN'S PARK VIEW

THE PARADE COMING FROM QUEEN'S PARK VIEW TO BRADFORD STREET ACROSS 'THE BANK', WHERE THE SHOPS NOW STAND ▼

The Choir and The Bells

A Choirboy Remembers

At Easter the Rector, Canon Sarson, would remove every three penny bit (or Joey) that was on the collection plate and share them among the choirboys. We each received a fresh egg as well.

Summertime meant the annual choir trip to the seaside—usually Llandudno! We used to enjoy this trip very much , except on one occasion, when, on the return trip, I was told I had to join the men's choir as my voice had broken.

Every Christmas the choirboys would visit the wards of the Old City Hospital on Hoole Lane to sing carols. Afterwards we had tea with the matron (who ruled the hospital with an iron fist) and then on to the pantomime at the Royalty Theatre in City Road, which first opened its doors on 23rd December 1882 with the pantomime, Aladdin.

Don Scarl

PHOTO—GILLIAN BROWN

▲ HANDBRIDGE CHURCH CHOIR C1925 (AT THE RECTORY)
SOME OF THE PERSONS SHOWN:
BACK BY RIGHT HAND DOOR POST: MR ROBERTS, THE VERGER
MIDDLE ROW (SEATED) CENTRE: REV A B RITCHIE, RECTOR, AND REV R L OWEN, CURATE.
CHOIRBOYS
MIDDLE ROW FROM THE LEFT: NO 1—GEORGE TAYLOR, NO 4—HAROLD PRITCHARD, NO 7—FRED RICHARDS, NO 9—TOM GREATBANKS
FRONT ROW, ON THE LEFT: 'NATTIE' CAMPBELL

Another Memory

Death of Mrs Ledsham, whose husband took part in the ringing of the first peal of bells in the tower of St Mary's, Church, Handbridge, on its opening in 1887.

Chester Chronicle 1st January 1944

ST MARY'S BELL ▶
RINGERS C1932
JAMES SWINDLEY, WHO WITH HIS FATHER MADE THE EASTGATE CLOCK, IS ON THE FRONT ROW, THIRD LEFT

THE CHURCH POSSESSES A FINE PEAL OF EIGHT BELLS CAST BY THE WHITECHAPEL FOUNDRY AND REHUNG IN 1979.

PHOTO—GWEN SHALLCROSS NÉE SWINDLEY

The earliest youth organisations were the Church Lads Brigade 1908—1930, followed by St Mary's Scouts, Guides, Cubs and Rovers c1920 with its Headquarters in Pyecroft Street. The Scouts bonfire, with its camp-fire singing, was always a popular pre-War event. So, too, were the Shrove Tuesday concerts of the Scouts and Guides in St Mary's Hall. After the War the group was revived, using the wooden hut on Eaton Road until 1974, when the Scouts moved to Westminster Park.

PHOTO—MARY MCHUGH

▲ ST MARY'S CHURCH BOYS' BRIGADE, ST MARY'S SCHOOL YARD, C1923

The 4th Chester Girl Guides Company

In 1920 I was asked to try to form a Guide Company in Handbridge—a depressing place in those days. The inaugural meeting took place in a room behind the Congregational Church. It was greeted by a howling mob of boys and girls at the door, which even the appearance of a kindly policeman did little to help. Rehearsals for a concert to raise money for uniforms were pandemonium, so was the concert! But gradually the meaning of guiding turned the rabble into proud wee guides and soon they were marching in a Company to any event in the town, to Empire Day services at the Cathedral, and to competitions with other Companies etc. I shall never forget our pride, as we marched for the first time with our own Colours to the Cathedral.

Sophie Hornby: Adapted from an Article in *A Handbridge Miscellany* 1964

PHOTO—LEN MORGAN

Another Memory

Mrs Betty Winder (neé Walls) of Devonshire Place and Eccleston Avenue was a Brownie, Guide and Ranger in St Mary's Company and a life-long supporter and leader of the Group. During the War she helped Mrs Sarson (the Rector's wife) to run the Forces Canteen in the wooden hut beside the Amphitheatre.

◄ 18TH CHESTER ST MARY'S CUB SCOUT SUMMER CAMP BROOKSIDE FARM, POULTON. 1991

On 10th January 1901 the foundation stone of a cottage home for pauper children was laid in Wrexham Road, beside the Overleigh Roundabout, by Joseph Pover JP. Previously these children had been housed and educated in the City Workhouse, Hoole Lane, which was considered to be inappropriate. To fund the project a loan of £6500 was raised; the Duke of Westminster rented the land and his architect, T M Lockwood, designed the Children's Home which opened in 1901.

Discipline of the Paupers

Art. 22. The boys and girls who are inmates of the workhouse shall, for three of the working hours, at least, every day, be respectively instructed in reading, writing, arithmetic, and the principles of the Christian Religion, and such other instruction shall be imparted to them as shall fit them for service and train them to habits of usefulness, industry, and virtue.

**Workhouse Rules,
Macclesfield Union—1841
Chester City Library**

PHOTO—LEN MORGAN

AFTER THE HOME CLOSED IN 1958, THE PROPERTY WAS SOLD AS TWO HOUSES

St Mary's Parish

The Home was in the ecclesiastical Parish of St Mary's and the children attended St Mary's Infant School, Handbridge. The Rector of St Mary's Church, as Chairman of the Managers, assumed responsibility for their education and attendance at Sunday School. Catholic children were looked after by the Friars of St Francis' Church.

Christmas 1944

Canon A W Sarson, dressed as Father Christmas, accompanied by the Festival Queen (Miss Carol Morgan), handed out the children's presents. On Boxing Day, the Mayor and Mayoress attended the Home. In the evening, the children paid their customary visit to the pantomime at the Royalty Theatre. The Duke of Westminster supplied the Christmas tree.

Chester Chronicle

What a contrast to the regime 100 years earlier!

CRO/Z/TRU166

OTHER HOMES WERE BUILT AT DODLESTON, UPTON AND SAUGHALL, BUT THE CENTRAL HOME AT OVERLEIGH WAS THE LARGEST, OCCUPYING ONE ACRE OF LAND. THE HOME HAD SEPARATE BOYS' AND GIRLS' DAY ROOMS AND DORMITORIES, ROOMS FOR THE SUPERINTENDENT AND MATRON, AND A SICK ROOM.

Handbridge Congregational / United Reformed Church

PHOTO—LEN MORGAN

HANDBRIDGE CONGREGATIONAL / UNITED REFORMED CHURCH

The Church was erected in 1881 on a site donated by the 1st Duke of Westminster, who, in 1892, also donated land behind the church for the building of a Sunday School.

FOUNDATION STONE SET IN THE CHURCH HALL ▶

History

The Church owes its origin to the Rev Philip Oliver, an evangelical clergyman who in 1796, began preaching services and started a Sunday school at premises in Greenway Street. Early in the 19th century John Hope and John Evans, members of the Queen Street Chapel, came to give leadership, and services continued throughout the century. In 1876 a church of thirty members was formed as a separate entity and this was the official date of the foundation of Handbridge Congregational Church.

By then, the old chapel premises in Greenway Street had become too small and a new chapel to seat 400 was built in 1881 (photograph left). Mr H T Higgins was its first minister with thirty nine members. It became the United Reformed Church in 1972. From 1985 Handbridge was established as a joint pastorate with St Andrew's URC in Newgate Street.

PHOTO—LEN MORGAN

THIS STONE WAS LAID BY MR EDWARD HUGHES, ON BEHALF OF THE TEACHERS AND SCHOLARS MAY 4TH 1892.

PHOTO—OBSERVER

THE START, IN MARKET SQUARE, OF THE HANDBRIDGE CHAPEL PROCESSION AROUND CHESTER IN 1928
IN THE BACKGROUND IS THE FORMER KING'S SCHOOL (NOW BARCLAY'S BANK)

Social Events

The Church has always been a lively centre for social events for adults and children. On New Year's Day, 1902, for instance, 'the Congregational Church held a most successful tea party; the Rev William Jones presided. Songs were sung by members of the Brython Choir.'

Chester Chronicle 4th January 1902

HANDBRIDGE CONGREGATIONAL SUNDAY SCHOOL ROSE QUEEN—1968 ▲
START OF THE HCSS PARADE OUTSIDE THE CHAPEL
LORRY LOANED BY MR BOBBY COXEN
(THE COTTAGES IN THE BACKGROUND HAVE SINCE BEEN DEMOLISHED)

MEMBERS OF THE CHURCH PRESENT A LIGHT OPERA, "ZURIKA" ▲
24TH TO 25TH SEPTEMBER 1952

▲ LEFT TO RIGHT:
BRENDA ROBERTS; ROSE QUEEN, MARY NIXON;
PRINCESS, (UNKNOWN);
SUSAN MEACOCK; MAXINE COXEN; SUSAN
MORGAN; SUSAN OWEN

▲HCSS ROSE QUEEN—1968
THE ROSE QUEEN AND HER 'COURT'

◄ CONGREGATIONAL CHAPEL
FANCY DRESS PARTY
HELD IN THE GARDENS OF GREENBANK—1965

LEFT TO RIGHT:
FREDDY HEDLEY; SUSAN TATLER; JOHN ROSEDALE
(MASKED); DOROTHY COLLEY; UNKNOWN ; PHILIP
MORRIS: UNKNOWN ; UNKNOWN ; SUSAN
MORGAN; JOHN ROSE; PETER MORGAN.

The Old Cemetery, Handbridge

Opened in 1850, Overleigh cemetery is an example of a Victorian burial ground, planned with winding footpaths, shrubs, trees and a lake with swans. All the original buildings and lake have gone. The WW I burials number 130 (12 in a separate plot). The 1939—45 burials total 71.

THE LAY-OUT OF OVERLEIGH CEMETERY

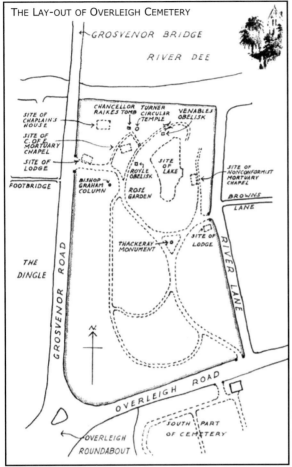

Interesting Graves

WILLIAM AYRTON
1850
THE FIRST PERSON TO BE BURIED IN THE CEMETERY

MARY JONAS
1890
MOTHER OF 33 CHILDREN (15 SETS OF TWINS)
WINNER OF A NATIONAL MAGAZINE COMPETITION TO FIND THE LADY WHO HAD CONTRIBUTED MOST TO THE POPULATION OF THE EMPIRE▼

▲ **RICHARD PRICE**
1960
CARVING OF THE GROSVENOR BRIDGE, RIVER DEE AND SALMON FISHING BOAT

Robert Newstead FRS, the renowned archaeologist, lived opposite the verger's house of St Mary's Church. He was Rector's Warden. **John Douglas** is buried a few yards from **Thomas Meakin Lockwood**, the two Victorian architects responsible for so many of Chester's fine buildings. **Edward Langtry** (right), the former husband of Lillie Langtry, mistress of King Edward VII, died in Chester on 16th October 1897, from a fall on board ship, travelling from Ireland to Holyhead. High on a bank lies the simple grave of a Chester girl from Liverpool Road, **Marjory Anne Tucker**, Women's Royal Air Force, killed by a train at Sealand Station on 31st August 1918, three months before the Armistice. Other gravestones tell of **Thomas Appleyard** (left), a builder remembered in Appleyard's Lane; **John Trainer,** a fireman, whose son and grandson both died at sea aged 20, one in 1882, the other in 1912; **William Biddulph Cross,** who took ten years to make his own coffin from thousands of matchboxes. It was lit inside by a battery. He died on 5th September 1905 aged 85.

PHOTO—LEN MORGAN

PHOTO—LEN MORGAN

LEN MORGAN CONDUCTS PUPILS FROM OVERLEIGH ST MARY'S SCHOOL AROUND THE OLD CEMETERY, HANDBRIDGE.
11TH MARCH 1994 (OPPOSITE PAGE) ▶

▼ THE 'CHEWING GUM' GIRL, MABEL FRANCES IRELAND BLACKBURN, DIED 13 NOVEMBER 1869, AGED 3½ YEARS. LOCALLY KNOWN AS THE CHEWING GUM GIRL, SUPPOSEDLY TO DISCOURAGE CHILDREN FROM SWALLOWING CHEWING GUM: IN FACT, SHE DIED OF WHOOPING COUGH. ALARNA MORGAN (LEN'S GRAND-DAUGHTER) SITS BESIDE MABEL'S GRAVE. ▼

PHOTO—IAN BIRCHENOUGH

PHOTO—LEN MORGAN

Overleigh New Cemetery, opened in 1879

The death of Mrs Coplestone (91), who was interested in Art, gave the New Cemetery an Eric Gill sculpture (St Francis of Assisi). He came to Chester to supervise its erection.

Chester Chronicle
11th August 1945

THE COPLESTON(E) FAMILY GRAVE ▶

PHOTO—LEN MORGAN

ERIC GILL (1882—1940), A SCULPTOR OF INTERNATIONAL REPUTE, IS BEST REMEMBERED FOR HIS 'STATIONS OF THE CROSS' IN WESTMINSTER CATHEDRAL AND HIS TYPEFACES, INCLUDING 'GILL SANS', USED IN THIS FRAME, (ORIGINALLY PRODUCED FOR THE LONDON AND NORTH EASTERN RAILWAY BEING USED FOR ALL SIGNS, ADVERTISING, AND TIMETABLES), AND 'PERPETUA'.

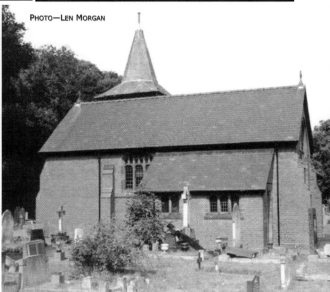

PHOTO—LEN MORGAN

GREEK ORTHODOX CHURCH, OVERLEIGH CEMETERY ▲
THE COMMUNITY OF ST BARBARA STARTED HERE IN 1985

PHOTO—LEN MORGAN

Catholics

There are no Catholic churches in Handbridge or Queen's Park, so worshippers attend either St Francis' or St Werburgh's churches.

St Francis' Church—designed by the Liverpool architect James O'Bryne

FROM A POSTCARD—COURTESY PETER BAMFORD

ST FRANCIS' CHURCH AND FRIARY c1904
THE CHURCH AND FRIARY OPENED 29TH APRIL 1875
(NOTE THE TRAMLINES)

The Church contains the shrine of St John Plessington, born near Garstang, Lancashire. He was chaplain to the Massey family at Puddington Hall in 1670. During the anti-Catholic agitation at the time of the alleged 'Popish Plot', he was arrested, imprisoned at Chester Castle, tried and condemned to death. He was hanged, drawn and quartered at Barrelwell Hill, Boughton, on 19th July 1679.

The Singing Friar

PHOTO—REV FRANCIS MAPLE

Rev Francis Maple OFM, Parish Priest and Community Guardian, since 1997; born in India, he was awarded the MBE for his charity work; writer and broadcaster—'Stars on Sunday'; gold disc, 1988—'Old Rugged Cross'; played at Drury Lane Theatre and the Liverpool Empire among others – and still going strong!

THE HIGH ALTAR SHOWING THE CALVARY AND THE STATUES OF FRANCISCAN SAINTS. LEFT IS THE STATUE OF ST AUGUSTINE AND RIGHT THAT OF ST PATRICK, THE APOSTLES OF ENGLAND AND IRELAND RESPECTIVELY.

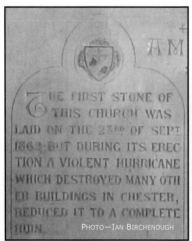

PHOTO—IAN BIRCHENOUGH

A TRIUMPH OVER ADVERSITY
BEFORE THE CHURCH WAS COMPLETED, THE ORIGINAL CONTRACTOR WENT BANKRUPT, AN EARTHQUAKE IN CHESTER IN OCTOBER 1863 BROUGHT DOWN THE EAST GABLE AND ON 3RD DECEMBER, A HURRICANE DESTROYED THE REST!

PHOTO—PETER BAMFORD

PHOTO—JOHN PARK

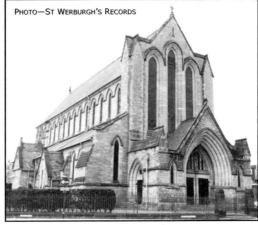

PHOTO—ST WERBURGH'S RECORDS

OPENED 13TH JULY 1876—THE FIRST TIME IN 1500 YEARS THAT A PAPAL LEGATE HAD STAYED IN CHESTER

King Alphonso XIII

1st December 1907: His Majesty, Alphonso, King of Spain, attended the 11 o'clock mass and gave £5 to the Building Fund, needing £4000 for the completion of the church.

Chester Catholic 1958/9

THE CONSECRATION OF BISHOP JOHN ▶
MURPHY AS CO-ADJUTOR BISHOP OF
SHREWSBURY 25TH FEBRUARY 1948.
BISHOP MURPHY LATER BECAME ARCHBISHOP OF
CARDIFF AND DIED IN 1995

PHOTO—ST WERBURGH'S RECORDS

PHOTO—CHESTER CATHOLIC 1959

THE FUNERAL OF CANON HUGH WELCH (62) ▲
11TH AUGUST 1959
THE CORTEGE, WHICH INCLUDED THE BISHOP OF
SHREWSBURY, RT REV DR J A MURPHY (RIGHT, IN
MITRE) PREPARES TO LEAVE FOR CHESTER OLD
CEMETERY. ONE OF THE COFFIN BEARERS WAS MR
DOWD, HEAD OF ST BEDE'S SCHOOL.

CANON WELCH, RECTOR OF ST WERBURGH'S ▶
FOR 15 YEARS AND A PRIEST FOR 35 YEARS.
AT 18, HE JOINED THE WELCH REGIMENT, WAS
WOUNDED AT BETHUNE IN 1918 AND TAKEN PRISONER.

CHESTER CATHOLIC

Rev Peter M Sharrocks

PHOTO—REV P M SHARROCKS

Father Peter Sharrocks, born 1951 in Stockport and educated at St Bede's College, Manchester and Ushaw College, Durham, was ordained priest for the Diocese of Shrewsbury in 1975. He was appointed Parish Priest at St Werburgh's in 1992, after serving at St Theresa's, Blacon, (1986—92) and in Kenya (1981—86).

121

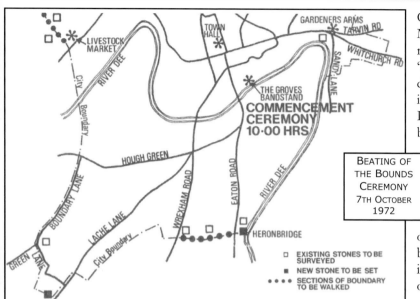

BEATING OF THE BOUNDS CEREMONY 7TH OCTOBER 1972

On Saturday 7th October 1972 the Mayor, Alderman C N Ribbeck, revived the ancient ceremony of 'beating the bounds', a custom dating from Anglo-Saxon times but in abeyance locally since World War I. The origin of this custom was to beseech God's blessing on parish lands for the coming harvest. However, before the days of maps, the ceremony also served to define the parish boundaries.

It was also the custom on occasions to whip or bump small boys on the actual boundary stones, in order to impress the boundaries on the minds of parishioners.

Accompanied by the sword and mace bearer, the Mayor left The Groves by river cruiser for Handbridge, as was done in 1913. There, the Mayor set the first of six new inscribed boundary stones, before leading the procession across fields and woodland to the Wrexham Road. This stretch of the parish boundary has remained unaltered for hundreds of years and includes several old boundary stones (some laid in 1785).

THE MAYOR OF WREXHAM, COUNCILLOR MRS WILLOW WILLIAMS, AND THE LORD MAYOR OF CHESTER, MRS MARGARET BYATT, 'BUMPING' LEWIS NORMAN AGED 8 ▶

The 1994 Ceremony

In 1994 the Lord Mayor of Chester, Councillor Margaret Byatt, her Consort, Mr Peter Byatt, the Sheriff of Chester, Councillor Elizabeth Bolton, and a party of VIPs, including the Mayor and Mayoress of Wrexham and Alderman C N Ribbeck, again re-enacted the ceremony. Three boundary stones were 'marked' at Threapwood (Sarn Bridge), Agden and Farndon with the traditional words …

'I, Margaret Byatt, Lord Mayor of the City of Chester, do hereby declare that this stone well and truly marks the boundary of the City of Chester at this point.

May the citizens of this parish enjoy good health, long life and prosperity.

God Save the Queen!'

The selected child was 'bumped' and the Bumper of Ale was passed round.

Queen's Park

PHOTO—HERITAGE CENTRE CH2073

CONSTRUCTION OF THE NEW SUSPENSION BRIDGE
OPENED APRIL 1923

Queen's Park – The Beginnings

Queen's Park was planned by Enoch Gerrard, the foundation stone of the first house being laid in July 1851. James Harrison, the well-known architect, was responsible for the design and layout of some of the houses and, in 1852, 'this picturesque, finely elevated and extensive estate'* was linked to Chester with a suspension bridge across the River Dee.

*Chester Chronicle—19th April 1851

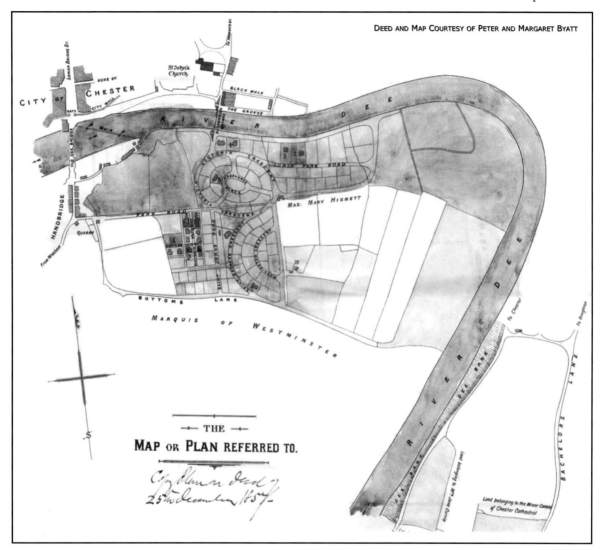

DEED AND MAP COURTESY OF PETER AND MARGARET BYATT

THE DEED (BELOW) SHOWS THAT, IN 1857, MOST OF THE LAND FOR THE NEW QUEEN'S PARK ESTATE HAD BEEN BOUGHT OR FINANCED BY THE COTTON MANUFACTURING FIELDEN FAMILY OF TODMORDEN, LANCASHIRE, WHO IMPOSED VERY RESTRICTIVE CONDITIONS E.G. '... TO BE RENTED OR SOLD ONLY TO RESPECTABLE FAMILIES ...' AND '... NO USE OF THE LAND FOR PURPOSES ... SUCH AS A ... MONASTERY OR NUNNERY...'.

Abstract of the Title of *John Ashton* ~~Messrs. SAMUEL~~ FIELDEN ~~and *Esq*~~ rc ~~JOHN FIELDEN~~ to the Queen's Park and Tentry Heyes and other estates situate in the city of Chester

25th December, 1857.

AS TO THE BOTTOMS FARM ESTATE BACHELORS' LANE AND BACHELORS' BUTT GORSTY BOTTOM OR HILL FIELD GORSTY MEADOW BOTTOM ESTATES AND MOIETY OF TENTRY HEYES ESTATE

Indenture of Conveyance of this date made between SAMUEL FIELDEN of Centre Vale Todmorden in the county of Lancaster merchant JOHN FIELDEN of Centre Vale aforesaid merchant and JOSHUA FIELDEN of Stansfield Hall in Todmorden merchant of the first part THOMAS WARNER of the city of Manchester in the county of Lancaster sharebroker of the second part and THOMAS FIELDEN of the said city merchant (a widower) of the third part

QUEEN'S PARK, CHESTER.

THIS picturesque, finely elevated, and extensive ESTATE, situate on the South side of the RIVER DEE and immediately adjoining the City, with which a close communication has been lately established by the erection of one of DREDGE'S PATENT SUSPENSION BRIDGES, is within easy reach either by river or road of the magnificent Park and Estates of the Marquis of Westminster (EATON HALL) and the delightful Village of ECCLESTON. Queen's Park commands extensive views of the surrounding country, including the range of the Welsh Mountains, Beeston Castle, and the Peckforton Hills; and, on the other side, of the Dee Banks, City Walls, the Cathedral, and Castle. This estate, so remarkable for the salubrity of its atmosphere and its many advantages, having a substratum of Red Sand Stone; its extensive river frontage giving facilities for fishing, boating, &t; and being within 10 minutes' walk of the Cathedral; and as the Chester General Railway Station is within 15 minutes' walk, LIVERPOOL is distant only an hour's journey from Queen's Park. The property has been recently laid out in BUILDING LOTS for the erection of VILLA RESIDENCES, and will be sold either on chief rent or entirely freehold; Lithographic Plans of which, or further particulars may be obtained on application to Mr. HITCHEN, in the Park, at Chester; Messrs. ATKINSON, SANDERS, and ATKINSON, Solicitors, Norfolk-street, or Messrs. GOLDSMITHS, Architects, Bond-street, MANCHESTER.

Chester Chronicle 19th April 1851

▼ A MAP (WHOSE DATE IS NOT KNOWN), SHOWING THE LOCATIONS OF QUEEN'S PARK FARM, QUEEN'S PARK BREWERY AND DERBY COTTAGE (MODERN LAYOUT ADDED)

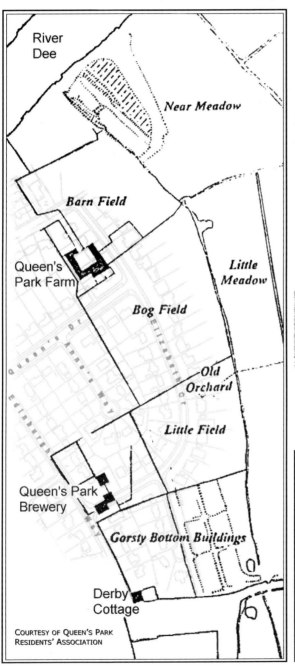

COURTESY OF QUEEN'S PARK RESIDENTS' ASSOCIATION

BELOW—TWO VIEWS OF QUEEN'S PARK FROM THE CITY WALLS C1850

STRANGER'S HANDBOOK TO CHESTER—1856

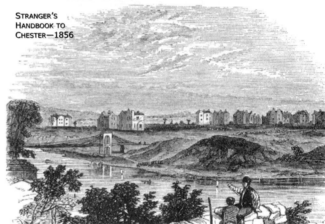

▼ DERBY COTTAGE DATING FROM BEFORE 1845.

PHOTO—RICHARD TOWNDROW

125

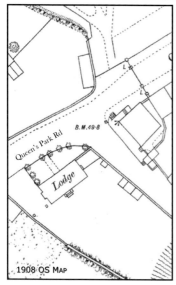

1908 OS Map

PHOTO—LEN MORGAN

Queen's Park Road was the private entrance for residents of Queen's Park. The Lodge (above right) was built in 1901 and demolished in 1988 to make way for retirement flats (below). There used to be a gate across the road, which is shown on the map above as a line across the road marked with two L's; the stump of its gatepost (Right) can be seen under the hedge on the opposite side of the road to Queen's Park View.

PHOTO—LEN MORGAN

PHOTO—LEN MORGAN

PHOTO—LEN MORGAN

▲ Queen's Park House Retirement Flats: built on the sites of the Lodge and Moore & Brocks Builders Supply Merchants.

Abbeyfield House Retirement flats: ▶ originally the Corona Pop Works stood on this site, which was later developed as a Kwik Save Supermarket.

PHOTO—LEN MORGAN

The Suspension Bridges — 1852 and 1923

The first suspension bridge was built by Enoch Gerrard in 1851, to link the new development in Queen's Park to the City. The bridge, costing £850, was opened in September 1852.

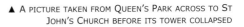

▲ A PICTURE TAKEN FROM QUEEN'S PARK ACROSS TO ST JOHN'S CHURCH BEFORE ITS TOWER COLLAPSED

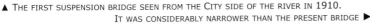

▲ THE FIRST SUSPENSION BRIDGE SEEN FROM THE CITY SIDE OF THE RIVER IN 1910.
IT WAS CONSIDERABLY NARROWER THAN THE PRESENT BRIDGE ▶

New Suspension Bridge. 1923.

In the presence of a large public gathering, the Mayor of Chester (Mr. Arthur Walls) performed the ceremony of opening the new Suspension Bridge. The bridge stands on the site of the old structure, which was demolished last autumn on account of its dangerous condition. The approximate cost will be £8000. Mr. J A Fielden gave a contribution of £4000.

The approach in the Groves was thronged with people, while others viewed the proceedings from the decks of several crowded launches. A space at the entrance on the north side was reserved for a number of privileged spectators. The members of the Corporation, Magistrates and officials assembled at St John's Parish Room, whence they walked in formal procession past the Grosvenor Park and down the steps to the bridge.

The Observer 21st April 1923 (Ch 213149)

PHOTO—CHRISTINE ROBINSON

THE SECOND SUSPENSION BRIDGE IN 1925 (LEFT) ▼ AND 1987 (RIGHT) ▼
THE ORIGINAL BRIDGE WAS DEMOLISHED ON ACCOUNT OF ITS DANGEROUS CONDITION IN 1922. THE GRACEFUL NEW BRIDGE HAS A SPAN OF 277 FEET AND IS 417 FEET LONG.

PHOTO—POST CARD

PHOTO—COURTESY OF LEN MORGAN

PHOTO—COURTESY OF MARTIN MEREDITH

AN AERIAL VIEW OF HANDBRIDGE AND QUEEN'S PARK TAKEN IN 1938

ON THIS PAGE:
TOP: THE SUSPENSION BRIDGE; WESTERN COMMAND (UNDER CONSTRUCTION); THE BOYS' GRAMMAR SCHOOL; QUEEN'S PARK
MIDDLE: THE ESTATE BETWEEN MEADOWS LANE AND APPLEYARDS LANE; THE (THEN NEW) ESTATE BETWEEN APPLEYARDS LANE AND ECCLESTON AVENUE
BOTTOM: EATON ROAD; ALLOTMENTS WITH PINFOLD LANE; FIELDS ON WHICH BELGRAVE PARK WAS TO BE BUILT.

ON THIS PAGE:
  TOP: THE HOUSES IN ST GEORGE'S CRESCENT; BOTTOMS LANE
MIDDLE: APPLEYARDS LANE; ALLINGTON LANE; ALLINGTON PLACE; BEESTON VIEW
BOTTOM: PINFOLD LANE WITH PINFOLD FARM (EXTREME LEFT)

AN AERIAL VIEW OF QUEEN'S PARK C1920 PROBABLY TAKEN BY WILL R ROSE, A PILOT IN WORLD WAR I.
NOTE THE ABSENCE OF THE WESTERN COMMAND/CAPITAL BANK BUILDINGS (NOW HALIFAX BANK OF SCOTLAND)

Some Houses of Distinction

PHOTO—RICHARD TOWNDROW

▲ TENTRY HEYS, QUEEN'S PARK ROAD
IN THE PARISH TITHE MAP OF 1845 THE PLOT WAS GIVEN AS No 31 OCCUPIED BY WILLIAM HADDOCK. IN
1905/6 THE HOUSE WAS OCCUPIED BY H S BLECKLEY

A document of 1394 states: *'Tentray Hayes - a place of land upon which stands the Tentoria of our lord the king, belonging to his fulling mills of Dee.'*

The Origin of Tentry Heys

The fulling mills in Mill Street, Handbridge, 'fulled' the woollen cloth (ie the cloth was puddled about in water and Fuller's earth to 'felt' it, making it close and waterproof). It was then stretched into shape on a frame of tenter hooks at Tentray Hayes.

This is the origin of the phrase 'to be on tenterhooks', as someone being in a state of anxious suspense, stretched like the cloth on the tenter. (The word originates from the Latin tendere — *to stretch).*

MANOR HOUSE,
2 QUEEN'S PARK ROAD
WAS BUILT IN 1852. THE
FIRST OWNER WAS
MR A WILLIAMS
IN 1916 THE HOUSE WAS
BOUGHT BY MRS MARY
DAVIES WHOSE DAUGHTER,
EMILY, AND HUSBAND,
GORDON JACOB (TIMBER
MERCHANT), SOLD IT IN
1968 TO ALEC AND IRMA
NEWTON.
THE HOUSE SUFFERED SOME
BOMB DAMAGE IN WORLD
WAR II.

PHOTO—RICHARD TOWNDROW

ST. JOHN'S ROAD. 1905/6

1	{ Griffiths, Mrs., { Griffiths, J.	*Elmhurst*
3	Nicholls, W. A. M.,	*Morwenstowe*
2	Miller, Hugh,	*Kilwinning*
4	Lucas, A. W., F.G.S.	
6	Golder, Miss	
8		
10	Holland, W.,	*Ashwood*
12	Taylor, G.	
14	Webster, M. S.	
16	Taylor, Mrs. J.	
	{ Jordan, Mrs.	*Fernhouse*
	{ Lockwood, Mrs. T. M.	

(widow of the celebrated architect
(see page 118)).

10 ST JOHN'S ROAD ▶
THE DESIGN OF THE HOUSE
(WHICH DATES FROM 1858) IS
ATTRIBUTED TO JAMES
HARRISON (ARCHITECT). HE
ALSO DESIGNED THE OTHER
SEMI-DETACHED VILLAS, 4,6
AND 8. IN JULY 1908 THE
FOUR HOUSES WERE APPROVED
AS STATUTORY LISTED
BUILDINGS.

PHOTO—SUSAN SMITH

VICTORIA PATHWAY, 1905/6

East		West	
2	Dutton J. R. *Ferndale*	1	Cameron-Davies W. L.
4	Eastwood Mrs	3	Room Mrs C. E.
6	Thompson L. A.	5	Farrell Mrs
8	Hornby Mrs H. A.	7	Barnett S.
10	Barrington Miss	9	Smith R. F.
12	Lloyd E.	11	Cotgreave J. H.
14	Bee A. *Glenroy*	13	Hughes E.
16	Moss Mrs	15	Hannon Miss
18	Smith E. L.	17	Dutton F. W.
20	Hughes Mrs W. *Southend*	19	Henderson J. E.

PHOTO—EMMA MOODY

VICTORIA PATHWAY WAS BUILT ▶
BETWEEN 1852 AND 1855.
THE LISTED HOUSES WERE PROBABLY
DESIGNED BY JAMES HARRISON AND THE EVEN
NUMBERS BUILT FOR THE 2ND MARQUIS OF
WESTMINSTER.

FROM LIME GROVE (1852) TO LINDEN GROVE (1997) VIA TAVENOR TOWERS (1983) ▶

THIS HANDSOME RIVERSIDE VILLA AT 7 LOWER PARK ROAD WAS BUILT IN 1852 BY FRANCIS AYLMER FROST, A WEALTHY CORN MERCHANT, FOR HIS SON ROBERT AS A WEDDING PRESENT. BETWEEN 1983 AND 1997, ANTHONY AND LYNNE MASSEY NAMED IT TAVENOR TOWERS AND USED ITS 15 BEDROOMS AND ITS PERIOD RECEPTION ROOMS AS 'BED AND BREAKFAST' ACCOMMODATION. THE HOUSE HAS NOW REVERTED TO ITS FORMER NAME. (LINDEN = LIME TREES IN GERMAN CF UNTER DEN LINDEN, A FAMOUS STREET IN BERLIN).

PHOTO—RICHARD TOWNDROW

REDCLIFF (1852)

PHOTO—RICHARD TOWNDROW

▲ 13, 15 (WHISPERS) & 17 (LIME GROVE COTTAGE), LOWER PARK ROAD (FORMERLY PART OF REDCLIFF)

NEXT DOOR TO LIME GROVE, **REDCLIFF** WAS ALSO BUILT IN 1852 BY FRANCIS AYLMER FROST FOR HIS OTHER SON, THOMAS GIBBONS FROST. IN 1869, THOMAS BECAME MAYOR OF CHESTER (THE YEAR IN WHICH THE TOWN HALL WAS BUILT AND FOR WHICH HE WAS KNIGHTED). HE EMPLOYED A COOK, BUTLER, PAGE, LADY'S MAID, NURSE, THREE MAIDS AND A COACHMAN. AFTER HIS DEATH AND THAT OF HIS WIFE, REDCLIFF WAS LET IN 1907 TO THOMAS COOPER, WHO BOUGHT THE FREEHOLD IN 1911 FOR HIS DAUGHTER, ANNIE. SHE LIVED THERE UNTIL HER DEATH IN 1978 AND IS STILL REMEMBERED BY LOCAL RESIDENTS. SUBSEQUENTLY, PART OF THE HOUSE WAS CONVERTED INTO APARTMENTS (ABOVE).

PHOTO—RICHARD TOWNDROW

▲THE CHALET AND THE MOUNT SOUTH CRESCENT ROAD

EARLY VICTORIAN VILLA, 5 VICTORIA CRESCENT ▼

PHOTO—RICHARD TOWNDROW

PHOTO—RICHARD TOWNDROW

PHOTO—LEN MORGAN

PHOTO—ARCHITECTS BENEVOLENT SOCIETY
PERMISSION OF HRH THE DUKE OF GLOCESTER

▲ THE SIGN, BY THE ARTIST MICHAEL JOHNSON, WAS COMMISSIONED BY CLAVERTON COURT (ARCHITECTS BENEVOLENT SOCIETY) AND INCORPORATES A SQUARE BRONZE PLAQUE CAST BY PHIL BEWES, A LOCAL SCULPTOR.

THE SIGN IS CONSTRUCTED IN STAINLESS STEEL AND BRONZE AND CONTAINS THE ORIGINAL PLAQUE, TOGETHER WITH IMAGES OF ARCHITECTURAL EQUIPMENT C1944, (ADJUSTABLE SET-SQUARE, COMPASSES, DRAWING PENS, AND PENCILS).

◀ HRH THE DUKE OF GLOUCESTER KG GCVO VISITED CLAVERTON COURT RECENTLY.

MR CHRIS COWEN, VICE-PRESIDENT OF THE SOCIETY, PRESENTED CENTENARIAN MRS NELLIE PICKERING TO HIS ROYAL HIGHNESS DURING HIS VISIT, 'WHICH HE MUCH ENJOYED'.

Thanks to Queen's Park Residents Association (founded in 1978), whose booklet, *A Brief History of Queen's Park, Chester* (January 2001), contains a wealth of information about Queen's Park.

PHOTO—COURTESY OF THE CLEEVES FAMILY

PHOTO—COURTESY OF THE CLEEVES FAMILY

CHAIRMAN OF THE CITY HOUSING COMMITTEE, LT COL F R CLEEVES OBE TD (1898—1988) AT WORK ON THE BUNGALOW, WHICH HE BUILT ALMOST SINGLE HANDED (1967—69) ON THE TENNIS COURT OF HIS HOUSE AT 28 ST GEORGE'S CRESCENT. A FORMER CITY SHERIFF, HE SERVED IN BOTH WORLD WARS.

Western Command (1907—1972).

The Army's Western Command stretched from Hadrian's Wall to Tewkesbury and included Lancashire, Cheshire, Wales and the West Midlands. Chester being a garrison city was the Headquarters of Western Command from 1907—1972. Originally based in Watergate House (built by Thomas Harrison in 1820), it moved into temporary accommodation at Richmond House, Boughton, in 1935. Under the General Officer Commanding in Chief Lt Gen H C Jackson, it occupied the new neo-Georgian building in Queen's Park on 1st October 1938 and remained there until 1972. Sir Brian Horrocks, a popular World War II general, was G O C in C (1946—47), followed by Lt Gen R H Haining CB DSO, son of the late Dr William Haining of Chester. The last Commander was Lt Gen Sir Napier Crookenden (1969—72), who was commissioned into the Cheshire Regiment in 1935. In 1972 the Royal Army Pay Corps (RAPC) took over the buildings, until the Ministry of Defence (MOD) closed the site in 1997.

PHOTO—LEN MORGAN

▲ AN AERIAL PHOTOGRAPH OF HQ WESTERN COMMAND TAKEN IN 1992
ITS DISTINCTIVE H SHAPE CAN BE SEEN BOTTOM RIGHT. THE SUSPENSION BRIDGE SPANS THE RIVER DEE WITH VICTORIA CRESCENT SWEEPING FROM CENTRE TOP TO CENTRE RIGHT. SOUTH CRESCENT ROAD (EITHER SIDE OF WHICH WERE PREVIOUSLY SITED MOD HUTS) SNAKES THROUGH THE TOP RIGHT QUARTER OF THE PHOTOGRAPH.

I Joined the ATS by Joan Rocke

On 3rd September 1939 (when my husband received his calling up papers for the TA), I, with some of my friends, joined the Auxiliary Territorial Service (ATS). About fifty of us assembled at the Drill Hall, were kitted out in khaki uniforms, tin hats and gas masks and marched through Chester to HQ, Western Command in Queen's Park, where we were welcomed by Gen Sir Brian Horrocks.

Many of the girls were billeted in houses commandeered in Queen's Park and around Chester. Once a week we all had to attend gas drill held beneath Western Command HQ. In the solid rock beneath HQ a replica of the offices above, complete with plumbing, air conditioning etc., had been constructed in the event of a direct hit.

My husband was posted to Bombay and I did not see him again for four years.

Soldier Magazine

The building of the new HQ Western Command in 1938/39 made work for hundreds of local men of all trades, mostly over call-up age. Men eager to work with picks and shovels, baskets, horses and carts, started to dig a large deep crater into the hillside. As war was declared in 1939, it was all speed to finish this large three section building, the Army moving in as the work progressed. In 1941, the building was camouflaged and a thin, dark grey wash paint was sprayed over the new bricks and stonework to prevent detection from the air.

In 1943 and 1944 secret military meetings were held in the underground section at Command HQ and only known in code to the Civil Defence military sections, in case the bridges were blown up. After the War the Civil Defence forces learned that these meetings were held between Winston Churchill, General Eisenhower and General de Gaulle.

Towards D-Day all streets and fields in Handbridge and Chester were stacked with military vehicles and with US Army trucks and tanks (which had come off the ships at Liverpool) to store them for the invasion of Europe.

Bess Savage, The Chester Chronicle
13th November 1998

PHOTO—CHESTER CHRONICLE

▲ HQ WESTERN COMMAND, QUEEN'S PARK
THE PICTURE SHOWS TEMPORARY WOODEN HUTS TO THE RIGHT OF THE ROADWAY.

MAP SHOWING MoD HUTS (SHADED) ▶
PRIOR TO WORLD WAR II, THE MoD BOUGHT LAND IN VICTORIA CRESCENT AND SOUTH CRESCENT ROAD, AND LEASED LAND BESIDE LOWER PARK ROAD FOR ARMY HUTS AND LARGE AIR-RAID SHELTERS. DURING THE WAR 4TH (CHESTER) ANTI-AIRCRAFT DIVISION, COMMANDED BY MAJ GEN H G MARTIN, WAS BASED IN LOWER PARK ROAD. THE HUTS REMAINED IN USE UNTIL THE LATE 1970S. CLAVERTON COURT OCCUPIES PART OF THIS LAND, SOLD IN 1980 BY THE MoD FOR HOUSING DEVELOPMENT. (SEE NEXT PAGE).

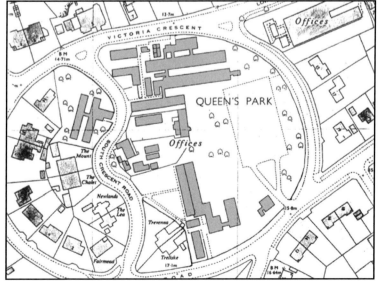

13 Splendid Individual Freehold Building Plots in Timbered Setting

at

QUEENS PARK CHESTER

PHOTO—MELLER BRAGGINS & CO

AVERAGE PLOT SIZE ¼ ACRE

FOR SALE BY AUCTION
AT THE GROSVENOR HOTEL, CHESTER
ON TUESDAY, 22nd JULY, 1980 AT 3 p.m.

Subject to Conditions of Sale herein contained

AUCTIONEERS:

Meller Braggins & Co

◄ PHOTOGRAPH AND TEXT FROM THE FRONT COVER OF MELLER BRAGGINS & CO BROCHURE FOR THE SALE OF MOD LAND IN 1980.
THE SITES BEING SOLD WERE FORMERLY OCCUPIED BY THE HUTS OF THE REGIMENTAL PAY OFFICE AND CAN BE CLEARLY SEEN WITHIN THE CIRCLE OF VICTORIA CRESCENT

Capital Bank – Bank of Scotland (now HBOS).

The MoD finally vacated the buildings of the former Western Command in 1997 and sold them to N W Securities for use as their Chester Head Office. The Company became the Capital Bank, then the Bank of Scotland, which recently merged to become the Halifax Bank of Scotland (HBOS).

CONSTRUCTION WORK IN APRIL 1998 ►

▼ ARCHITECTS' SKETCH OF THE NEW BUILDINGS 1997

PHOTO—LEN MORGAN

THE CHRONICLE

CAPITAL BANK

M:CORMICK ARCHITECTURE

A VIEW FROM THE RIVER MAY 1998 ▼

PHOTO—LEN MORGAN

Factfile (The Chronicle 19th September 1997)

The Capital Bank scheme, prepared by Saighton-based McCormick Architecture, retains the 1930s building.

It will increase its height, add a new building at right angles to it, and provide a gatehouse at the site entrance.

Altogether, there will be 10,158 square metres of floorspace, including offices, board room, dining room, staff restaurant, meeting rooms and a gymnasium.

Queen's Park Estate Company

Queen's Park Estate Company was formed in the 1930s by a group of Chester businessmen for the residential development of Queen's Park Farm (see page 125). The farmhouse, occupied by the Fishwick family, was located where Queen's Drive now joins Elizabeth Crescent. In a land exchange with Chester Corporation, the Company took land for building in Andrew Crescent and the Corporation took the field by 'The Meadows', on which the Queen's Park High School boathouse now stands. Just before World War II land was also sold to the War Department for huts.

After the Second World War the Company, which did not itself build the houses, laid out a series of roads (Queen's Drive, Edinburgh Way, the south side of Lower Park Road, Elizabeth Crescent and Andrew Crescent). It sold building plots either to private individuals or building contractors. The final developments in the 1980s were the last four houses on the south-west side of Lower Park Road.

QUEEN'S PARK FARM AND LIME GROVE COTTAGE IN 1946. ▶
REPLACING BOTTOMS FARM IN THE 1850S, QUEEN'S PARK FARM WAS DEMOLISHED IN THE EARLY 1960S TO MAKE ROOM FOR MORE HOUSING

PHOTO—HUGH ALDRED

Memories of a Teenage Maid
in St John's Road c1900

My grandmother, Isabella Day née Willetts, was born in 1888. During her teenage years she was a maid at 1 St John's Road, in service to two elderly maiden ladies.*

One day, when she was dusting in the parlour, she overheard the ladies speaking with consternation and dismay that they had heard that someone, owning a painting and decorating business, had bought a house nearby.

'Just fancy,' said one to the other, 'trades people moving into St John's Road!'

One of my grandmother's duties, when the ladies were going out, was to summon a cab. The horse-drawn cabs used to wait in file in Victoria Crescent. For this duty she had to remove her white cap and apron—it wasn't the 'done thing' for maids to be seen outside the house in uniform.

Pearl Evans, of 20 Elizabeth Crescent

*Probably the Sloane sisters.

In the 1881 census, a certain Hannah Sloane, aged 69, a widow, born in Ireland and whose occupation is listed as 'invested capital', was living at 1 St John's Road, along with her two daughters, Hannah (40) and Maria (38). Both daughters were single and had been born in Chester. A domestic servant, Jane Jones from Welshpool, also lived there.

By 1905 no Sloanes were living at this address. (Directory 1905/06)

Queen's Park and Handbridge can be proud of its association with Mr McAllister Turner, an internationally renowned artist who, for part of his life, lived and worked at 8 Victoria Pathway. Born in Mold in 1901, he first discovered his natural talent and love for art, when he sketched a Chester tram at the age of four during a visit with his mother. The sketch stayed with him throughout his career and was proudly exhibited by him in later life. He died in Chester aged 75.

On leaving school, Turner would walk to Chester to attend evening classes at the Chester School of Art (then in the Grosvenor Museum). Advised to follow a career in art by artist Sir John Lavery,

▲ Exhibiting his work to a group of young admirers

he went on to receive the prestigious Caldecott Memorial Prize for his work and exhibited his paintings, etchings and sculptures in London, New York, Buenos Aires and Patagonia. He was five times appointed President of the Royal Cambrian Academy and had an art gallery and studio for many years in Bonewaldesthorne's Tower on the City Walls in Chester. Perhaps his most outstanding achievement was his fourteen paintings of the Stations of the Cross dedicated to the Catholic Church in Hawarden, where he lived and worked for many years.

Text based on the contents of a scrap book of Mr R Martin, who kindly gave permission for the text and photographs to be used for publication.

Emma Stuart, Chester Heritage Centre

▼ The Duke of Edinburgh was so impressed with the work of McAllister Turner, that he requested one of his etchings for his own collection.

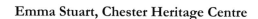

Photo—Ray Martin

▲ An etching by McAllister Turner

The Meadows

▲ THE MEADOWS IN FLOOD, TAKEN FROM THE CHESHIRE CONSTABULARY AEROPLANE, NOVEMBER 2000.

▼ THE LEGAL AGREEMENT TRANSFERRING THE LAND TO THE CITY

AN AGREEMENT made the *twenty eighth* day of *January* One thousand nine hundred and twenty six BETWEEN HARRY FAULKNER BROWN J.P. of 18 Curzon Park in the City of Chester Solicitor and LOUISA PHYLLIS BROWN J.P. his wife (hereinafter called "the Donors") of the one part and THE MAYOR ALDERMEN AND CITIZENS OF THE CITY AND COUNTY OF THE CITY OF CHESTER (hereinafter called "the Corporation") of the other part WHEREAS the Donors are desirous of presenting to the Corporation the lands situate at Queen's Park in the City of Chester and known as The Meadows or the Earl's Eye containing an area of 74·42 acres or thereabouts and delineated and shown edged pink on the plan hereto annexed (which said lands are hereinafter referred to as "the lands") for use as a public park recreation ground or lands for cricket football or other games and recreations in perpetuity AND WHEREAS the Corporation have in the present Session applied to the Minister of Health for a Provisional Order under the powers of the Public Health Act 1875 to enable them (inter alia) to acquire the lands otherwise than by agreement AND WHEREAS the parties hereto have agreed to enter into the agreements hereinafter contained NOW IT IS HEREBY AGREED by and between the parties hereto as follows:-

1.　——Failing agreement between the Corporation and the present owner of the land the Corporation shall use their best endeavours to obtain the said Provisional Order and the confirmation thereof by Parliament authorising them to acquire the lands for the purposes aforesaid.

Ferries Across The Dee

A popular recreation area for generations, The Meadows were given to the City in 1926 by Mr Harry Faulkner Brown J P and Louise Phyllis Brown, on condition that they were always to be for the use of the citizens for recreation.

A number of ferries operated across the Dee, including those established in the 19th century on the east bank of the river by The Red House Hotel (closed c1950) and The White House Hotel (closed 1971). These allowed patrons of the hotels to cross to and from the Meadows.

In 1947 the City Corporation started a ferry from Sandy Lane to the Meadows, using a rowing boat operating from May to September. This proved so popular that an additional ferry was introduced operating 10am—dusk, Whit to September. This was withdrawn in 1975, leaving the Sandy Lane ferry as the only survivor on the Dee.

Alan Sharp, 'Ferries of the Dee'

PHOTO—FRANK AUTY

PHOTO—MARTIN LAW-BRIGGS

PHOTO—TOM GARMORY

PHOTO—ADELE EDWARDS

TOP:
VIEW ACROSS THE RIVER
DEE FROM LOWER PARK
ROAD

CENTRE LEFT:
PARENTS IN WAITING!
THE PEN NORMALLY DOES
45 DAYS' SITTING, WHILE
THE COB PROTECTS ITS
TERRITORY.

CENTRE RIGHT:
ACROSS THE RIVER TO ST
PAUL'S CHURCH AND
BARRELWELL HILL

BOTTOM:
CATTLE GRAZING—THE
CHEAPEST AND BEST FORM
OF GRASSLAND
MANAGEMENT!

FRIENDS OF THE MEADOWS

The Friends of the Meadows

The Meadows (or the Earl's Eye) is an area of natural beauty with an associated wildlife, bordering the River Dee and classified as a Site of Biological Interest. The Friends of the Meadows was established in 1994, with the encouragement of Chester City Council, to support the management of the Meadows, as an area of local nature conservation and to provide facilities for quiet public recreation.

Chairman: Miss Adele Edwards
32 Elizabeth Crescent

PHOTO—TERESA KOSTIUK

WINNERS OF THE CHESTER 'CAMELOT CHALLENGE', ▶ FOR THE MOST INTERESTING COLLECTION OF RUBBISH (BOOTS, CRATES, EVEN A WHEELBARROW!).
   L TO R:
      ADELE EDWARDS; SUSIE HINGSTON; TERESA KOSTIUK (CAMELOT); CLLR LILIAN PRICE (MAYOR OF CHESTER); DEREK SMITH

THE END OF THE SPONSORED WALK FROM BANGOR-ON-DEE TO THE MEADOWS (32 MILES). MONEY WAS RAISED FOR A SEAT ON THE MEADOWS FOR THE ELDERLY. ▶

L TO R:
MARK WILLIAMS, DAVID NIELD (LORD MAYOR), ANN NIELD (LADY MAYORESS), ADELE EDWARDS, GRAHAME JONES, MIKE DIX, SARAH EALEY, CAROLINE EALEY (IN FRONT)

PHOTO—ADELE EDWARDS

THE ANNUAL ▶ MIGRATION TO THE MEADOWS *(RITA HIBBITT)*

Meadows Log

Aug　*46 swans counted in Sandy Lane area: cygnets now number three (two thought to have been killed by dogs when they ventured on or close to the bank).*

Fry observed again in shallows during warm spells.

Fishermen slowly returning, as fish stocks recover—but so does cormorant activity!

Oct　*Merlin, a small bird of prey, observed on several occasions at the foot of Pinfold Lane.*

Conservation volunteers at work on Gorsty Bank. Autumn lunchtime cruise aboard Mark Twain— raffle raised £215 for Claire House Hospice.

Autumn lecture, The Story of Chester's Swans *by Jackie Leech MBE at St Mary's Church Hall.*

Dec　*Hazel catkins already well formed in Bottoms Lane hedgerow. The Dee was high and fast flowing at the month's end*

PHOTO—ADELE EDWARDS

◄ CONSERVATION WORK ON THE MEADOWS. PLANTING TREES AND PRESERVING THE WILD LIFE OF SWANS, HERONS, MOORHENS, CORMORANTS AND DUCKS

OPERATION DEEP OCTOBER: (1996)

Operation Deep October was an exercise, designed to push the emergency services to their limits, in which a collision between a speedboat and the Lady Diana was simulated.

PHOTO—CHESTER CHRONICLE

More than 150 people played a part in an elaborately staged and frighteningly realistic drama, including members of the Queen's Park Residents' Association and Friends of the Meadows, as passengers of the *Lady Diana.*

PHOTO—CHESTER CHRONICLE

A Walk Around Handbridge

THE OLD DEE BRIDGE—A 1908 POST CARD

PHOTO—LEN MORGAN

PUPILS FROM QUEEN'S PARK HIGH SCHOOL
ON A LOCAL HISTORY PROJECT WITH LEN MORGAN

PHOTO—LEN MORGAN

▲ THE ENTRANCE TO HANDBRIDGE (LEFT) FROM CHESTER

The Old Dee Bridge was, until 1831, the only bridge across the Dee at Chester. Fordable at low tide (see p 10), the River was probably bridged by the Romans. Around here the sense of History is very noticeable.

Upstream from the bridge is the most photographed view of the river—the Groves with its bandstand, river-craft and concourse of people. In the distance is the Suspension Bridge, built in 1923 to replace the earlier bridge of 1852, linking the new suburb of Queen's Park to the City. Beyond this, leading to Eccleston and the lawns of Eaton Hall, was a favourite recreational stretch of the river in Edwardian times.

Downstream across the river can be seen the Castle and County Hall, the latter opened by the Queen in 1957. Gone are the gaol and the Dee mills. The mills, which in medieval times were granted a monopoly of the grinding of Chester's corn, were destroyed by fire in 1910 and replaced by a hydro electric power station in 1913.

PHOTO—LEN MORGAN

▲ THE GROVES WITH A PLEASURE BOAT AND THE BANDSTAND.

PHOTO—FROM THE OFFICIAL PROGRAMME OF THE OPENING OF COUNTY HALL

▲ COUNTY HALL IN 1957 TAKEN FROM EDGAR'S FIELD

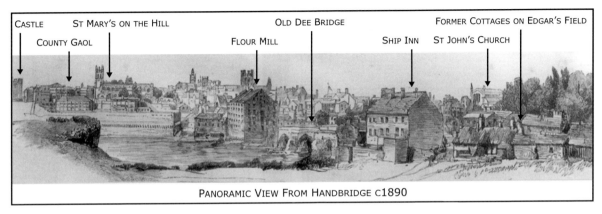

CASTLE   ST MARY'S ON THE HILL   OLD DEE BRIDGE   FORMER COTTAGES ON EDGAR'S FIELD

COUNTY GAOL   FLOUR MILL   SHIP INN   ST JOHN'S CHURCH

PANORAMIC VIEW FROM HANDBRIDGE c1890

PHOTO—COURTESY OF BRIAN COX

THE QUEEN IS SHOWN THE VIEW OF HANDBRIDGE

ON HER VISIT TO CHESTER TO OPEN COUNTY HALL, 11TH JULY 1957, HM THE QUEEN WAS SHOWN THE VIEW OF THE RIVER AND HANDBRIDGE.

◄ SEEN ESCORTING THE QUEEN DOWN THE STEPS OF COUNTY HALL IS ALDERMAN J WESLEY EMBERTON, JP, CHAIRMAN OF CHESHIRE COUNTY COUNCIL

▼ A VIEW OF HANDBRIDGE TAKEN FROM COUNTY HALL ABOUT THE TIME OF THE QUEEN'S VISIT. THE FORMER SALMON FISHERMEN'S HOUSES NESTLE BELOW ST MARY'S CHURCH. ON THE SKYLINE AT THE RIGHT IS THE WATER TOWER AND ON THE LEFT, IN EDGAR'S FIELD, THE BANDSTAND.

PHOTO—GARRY LESLEY

1959

The opening by HM the Queen sets the seal on many years of endeavour to provide a worthy seat of county government and centralised office accommodation for Departments.

The County Hall stands on a site previously occupied by ancient county buildings, including part of the Old Gaol. It adjoins, and is linked to, the Castle, built and used as a military stronghold … but long associated with the government of the people and the administration of justice.

From the steps the Queen would have seen 'a particularly fine view of many features of ancient Chester—the Dee Mills, Edgar's Field, the church of St Mary without-the -walls, the salmon fishing village of Handbridge and the old City walls.'

Official Programme of the Opening, 11th July 1957—Chester Library

Ahead lies the main street of Handbridge with its pubs and shops. Often destroyed by Danes, marauding Welshmen, and razed to the ground during the Civil War, Handbridge has no medieval buildings. Still prominent is the Ship Inn—an inn must have occupied this important site of toll, defence and passage for centuries.

The notorious 'Courts' were demolished 1926—28. In their places the Corporation built 207 houses and 12 shops. Chester Chronicle, 19th March 1927, reported:

'Residents of Broad Entry, Jones, Evans and Coach Courts have received notice on 10th March 1927 to quit within fourteen days, as they have been allotted a Council house on the new estate. Rent 11s 3d in advance. The key will not be handed over, unless a Medical Certificate is produced that you and your family have been disinfected.'

PHOTO—LEN MORGAN

▲ THE LIMESTONE POST IS A REMNANT OF THE TOLL BAR. TOLLS WERE ABOLISHED ON THE OLD DEE AND GROSVENOR BRIDGES ON 1ST JANUARY 1885

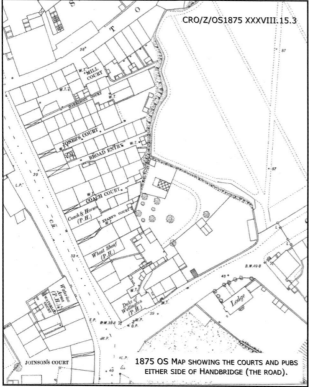

CRO/Z/OS1875 XXXVIII.15.3

1875 OS MAP SHOWING THE COURTS AND PUBS EITHER SIDE OF HANDBRIDGE (THE ROAD).

PHOTO—HERITAGE CENTRE CH2175

▲ THE CORNER OF MILL STREET AND HANDBRIDGE SHOWING ONE OF THE THREE HOUSES BUILT IN MILL STREET AND THE SHOPS AND FLATS BUILT IN HANDBRIDGE (THE ROAD) IN 1930.

◀ SOME OF THE COURTS BEING DEMOLISHED. THE ENTRANCE IN THE CENTRE OF THE PICTURE IS THAT TO 'JONES COURT'.
L T C ROLT (BORN 1910) (SEE P 85) 'WHEN PUSHING ME IN MY PRAM TOWARDS THE CITY, MY NURSE ALWAYS HURRIED PAST THIS SQUALID ROOKERY WITH AVERTED EYES, CLINGING TO THE OPPOSITE SIDE OF THE ROAD!' (AUTOBIOGRAPHY).

PHOTO—CHESTER CHRONICLE, 16TH JUNE 1928

Modern Shops

A variety of shops, selling a wide range of goods and services, cater for the needs of the local community, despite the competition of Chester's supermarkets.

PHOTO—LEN MORGAN

PHOTO—LEN MORGAN

PHOTO—IAN BIRCHENOUGH

POST OFFICE

CLOCKWISE FROM TOP LEFT:

- THE LOCAL GREENGROCER CARRYING ON FROM MRS WILD— SUE BLYTHIN GETTING READY FOR HALLOWEEN.

- PESCADOR FISHMONGERS, MEMBERS, ALONG WITH WEINHOLTS AND EDGES, OF THE CHESTER GUILD OF FINE FOOD AND WINE GUARANTEEING QUALITY AND SERVICE. AFTER A CAREER IN THE MERCHANT NAVY, AND AS A FISHERMAN IN FLEETWOOD AND DARTMOUTH, MARTIN DEARING (52) GAVE UP CATCHING FISH TO SELL THEM.

- AT THE CORNER IN THE EARLY PART OF THE CENTURY STOOD 'THE DUKE OF WELLINGTON' (DEMOLISHED IN THE LATE 1920S), CURRENTLY THE SITE OF MARTIN'S NEWSAGENTS.

- THREE SHOPS IN QUEEN'S PARK VIEW BUILT IN THE 1930S ON A SITE KNOWN LOCALLY AS 'THE BANK'. (SEE P 112)

- THE HANDBRIDGE SERVICE STATION AND A LITTLE FURTHER UP THE HILL THE CHERRY VALLEY CHINESE RESTAURANT AND THE LAUNDERETTE.

PHOTO—LEN MORGAN

PHOTO—LEN MORGAN

PHOTO—LEN MORGAN

◀ THE SWAINSON FAMILY OUTSIDE THEIR HOME, 88 BRADFORD PLACE, IN 1904
LEFT TO RIGHT:
JOHN; JAMES (FATHER); LILLE; JAMES; MABEL; JANE (MOTHER); ANNIE; ELLENOR.

88 BRADFORD PLACE TODAY ▼

PHOTO—LEN MORGAN

There is a place in Chester, which bears and has borne the name of 'Paradise' for several centuries. Situated in Handbridge, it consists of half a dozen cottages between Percy Road and the highway. It is reached by an unnamed passageway leading off Bottom (or Meadows) Lane. The 1881 census shows a stonemason living at No 6 with his wife and three children.

Mr W Brown, in an article on Chester street names, wondered whether the builder of the cottages was a wag, who gave to his property this delightful name to convey an idea of happiness to be enjoyed there. But this secluded spot was so named in the time of Henry VIII—long before the cottages were built.

The Cheshire Sheaf and
Archæological Journal vol. 13, 1936

PHOTO—WENDY MOORCROFT

▲ 'THE GREEN' HARTINGTON STREET 1933

PHOTO—HERITAGE CENTRE PHOTOSURVEY

▲ PARADISE IN 1968
NOW RETIREMENT HOMES HAVE BEEN BUILT THERE ▶
NOTE: WATER TOWER AND ST MARY'S SPIRE

PHOTO—LEN MORGAN

Handbridge Hill

Up Handbridge Hill towards Belgrave Place and Overleigh, the photographs show the changes during the 20th century.

PHOTO—LEN MORGAN

PHOTO—CHESTER CHRONICLE

TWO PICTURES OF THE HANDBRIDGE HILL TAKEN IN THE 1960S

▲ LOOKING DOWN TOWARDS QUEEN'S PARK ROAD, ON THE LEFT IS GREENWAY STREET WITH EDGE'S SHOP ABOVE IT AND WILD'S OLD SHOP BELOW. BELGRAVE PLACE IS ON THE RIGHT.

◄ LOOKING UP TOWARDS EATON ROAD AND OVERLEIGH ROAD (1950S), THE ENTRANCE TO BELGRAVE PLACE CAN BE SEEN AT THE EXTREME RIGHT.

PHOTO—LEN MORGAN

1991—THE COTTAGES SEEN ABOVE WERE REPLACED BY TOWN HOUSES IN 1977/78 ►
NOTE THE POST (BOTTOM LEFT) IS THE SAME IN BOTH PHOTOGRAPHS

LEN MORGAN SURVEYS THE CEMETERIES, SCHOOLS AND OPEN FIELDS OF HANDBRIDGE

PHOTO—AIRVIEWS (MANCHESTER) LTD. COURTESY OF NOEL ST JOHN WILLIAMS

ON THIS PAGE
TOP: THE DUKE'S DRIVE, CATHOLIC HIGH SCHOOL, PART OF THE NEW CEMETERY, OVERLEIGH ROUNDABOUT
BOTTOM: EATON ROAD, GREENBANK

ON THIS PAGE

TOP: OVERLEIGH ROAD, THE NEW CEMETERY WITH ST BARBARA'S CHURCH, THE OLD CEMETERY, THE RIVER DEE, THE WATER TOWER.

MIDDLE: OVERLEIGH ST MARY'S SCHOOL, WEST CHESHIRE COLLEGE, NETHERFIELD AND NETHERLEIGH HOUSES.

BOTTOM: THE FIELDS WHERE BELGRAVE PARK NOW STANDS.

PHOTO—LEN MORGAN

▲ THE REMODELLED BELGRAVE PLACE IN 1991 FROM THE SAME VIEWPOINT AS THE PICTURE BELOW RIGHT

BELGRAVE PLACE IN 1960 LOOKING OUT TOWARDS HANDBRIDGE. THE WHITE HORSE CAN BE SEEN FACING ON THE LEFT. ▶

THE VIEW OF BELGRAVE PLACE FROM THE MAIN ROAD, AS IT LOOKS TODAY. THE BEAUTIFUL DISPLAY OF TREES AND FLOWERS IS THE WORK OF KEN LEDWARD, FORMER HEAD GARDENER OF EATON HALL, WHO LIVES IN BELGRAVE PLACE ▼

PHOTO—LEN MORGAN

PHOTO—LEN MORGAN

PHOTO—LEN MORGAN

1999

1955

The Hand Family of Sty Lane (Greenway Street)

Descended from Thomas, Mayor of Chester 1658—9

A son, Thomas, Mayor 1701.

Matthew Ellis of Overleigh sold his house and lands in Handbridge to Hugh Hand (Cheshire Sheaf XLV 1950). Hugh, a husbandman, leased Paradise for 99 years from Matthew Ellis (Cheshire Sheaf 1936. 6775).

1812—Samuel Hand, shipwright of Virgin Street (Belgrave Place), was made a Freeman.

1833—Thomas Hand of Handbridge, a roper, died there.

1841 Census—his widow, Sophia lived in Overleigh. A son was living in Greenway Street/Sty Lane. Robert, 18 months old, died there.

1861 to 1901 Censuses—Hands living in Greenway Street.

Gillian Brown

2nd house left was No 54 (see p 17)   PHOTO—COURTESY OF MIKE PENNEY

1962

PHOTO—LEN MORGAN

1963

PHOTO—LEN MORGAN

TWO PICTURES OF THE JUNCTION WITH BROWN'S LANE BELOW: A PHOTOGRAPH (TAKEN IN THE 1880s) OF THE COTTAGES, WHICH WERE REPLACED IN 1896 BY THE MORE STYLISH GRADE II BUILDINGS, (LEFT). THEY WERE COMMISSIONED BY HUGH LUPUS, FIRST DUKE OF WESTMINSTER, AND DESIGNED BY JOHN DOUGLAS.

John Douglas *practised architecture in Chester from around 1855, until his death at 81 in 1911.*

1879   'Maypole' boundary wall railings
1887—88 Sexton's Cottage, St Mary's Church
1892—93 Re-slating St Mary's Church
1896—97 Cottages, 26—40 Overleigh Road
1898   Pinfold Lane Farm, Handbridge
1899   Houses, 65—67 Handbridge

'The Work of John Douglas'
by Edward Hubbard (Appendix II)

John Douglas lived at 33, Dee View (Dee Banks), Great Boughton. His mother, Mary (née Swindley), was born in Alford in 1792. Her father, John Swindley, was the village blacksmith at Eccleston. Until 1960 members of his family worked as smiths and metalworkers in Handbridge. Their most photographed creation was the iron framework for the Eastgate Clock.

PHOTO—MRS YORK

▲ OVERLEIGH ROAD JUST PAST THE RED LION IN 1955—THE COTTAGES HAVE ALL BEEN DEMOLISHED

PHOTO—CHESTER CHRONICLE

PHOTO—CHESTER CHRONICLE

◄ THE EATON ESTATE DEVELOPMENT, OVERLEIGH ROAD, 1971

Pyecroft Street (*Pie*=Magpie + *Croft*=Enclosed Field)

One of Handbridge's oldest streets, Pyecroft Street is currently designated a conservation area to protect its architecture. Properties on the East side comprise of an attractive terrace of double fronted artisans' cottages with added parlour built in the 1850s; for those houses on the West side, built in the 1860s, grants are available to residents, in order to restore the properties to their original state.

SALE

To be sold by Private Contract
'THE PYE CROFT'
land now in the occupation of
MRS LUNT, containing upwards of
12,000 square yards. This land is
admirably adaptable for the building of
cottages.

Chester Chronicle, 19th April 1851

PYECROFT STREET (WEST SIDE), 1980 ▶

PHOTO—CHESTER CHRONICLE

PICTURE—COURTESY OF TECH. GROUP, CHESTER CITY COUNCIL

PYECROFT STREET (EAST SIDE)

An Early 20th Century Memory of the Pyecroft Street Community

The boat builder, William Roberts, who lived at 55 Pyecroft House, was the great grandfather of Dilys Dowswell (now living at 9 Victoria Pathway, Queen's Park). In 1938—39, she lived with her great grandfather. (see p 60) She taught English at Love Street School and Queen's Park High School.

William Roberts related that they were surrounded by tradesmen artisans, who helped each other, such as Jimmy Harper (plumber), Mr Gibson (baker with Bollands), Mr Relish (builders), dressmakers, electricians etc.

'In this caring community, neighbour looked after neighbour in times of need', said 95 year old Mrs Moulton, who has lived all her life in Pyecroft Street.

1900—01 RESIDENTS' LIST
PYECROFT STREET

Phillipson & Golder's Directory for Chester

1	Barnett, F.	2	Edwards, W.
	St Mary's Mission House	2A	Robinson, R.
3	Jones, C.	4	Swindley, G
5	Saunders, J.	6	Nicholson, T.
7	Cotgreave, G.	8	Jones, W. D.
9	Jones, R.	10	Thomas, W. T.
11	Smith, Mrs.	12	Brown, H.
13	Reed, F. F.	14	Garratt, G. H.
15	Coffin, M. J.	16	Aspey, T.
17	Sullivan, Mrs.	18	Baker, J. J.
19	Griffiths, E.	20	Hayes, J.
21	Crosbie, C.	22	Croft, A. W.
23	Boden, J.	24	Povey, T.
25	Barnes, A.	26	Bithell, W. H.
27	Harper, J.	28	Gardener, H. T.
29	Buckley, J.	30	Keating, C.
31	Connor, Mrs., dressmaker	32	Dodd, J.
33	Dean, E.	34	Jones, Mrs. W., shopkeeper
35	Jones, H.	36	Lloyd, J. E.
37	Griffiths, G.	38	Richards, H.
39	Birch, J. H.	40	Johnson, J. L.
41	Brown, J.	42	Griffiths, S.
43	Edwards, J.	44	Woodcock, J.
45	Meredith, J.	46	Orrett, Mrs., nurse
47	Jarvis, L.	48	Newns, E.
49	Tapley, L.	50	Rathbone, S.
51	Whittingham, S.	52	Haddocks, Mrs.
53	Jones, R.	54	Reynolds, A.
55	Roberts, W.,	56	Swinnerton, W.
	Pyecroft house	58	Davenport, W.
		60	Peterson, J.
CHESTER LIBRARY		62	Paddock, J.

155

The opening of the Grosvenor Bridge to traffic in 1832 provided Chester with a second route to North Wales and the South. It also rendered the old road to Wrexham redundant and turned it into a pleasant village lane.

OLD WREXHAM ROAD IN THE 1960S (LEFT) SHOWING POWELL'S FARM AND, FROM THE SAME VIEWPOINT, IN 1990 (RIGHT)

OVERLEIGH ROAD AT THE JUNCTION WITH OLD WREXHAM ROAD IN THE 1950S (LEFT) AND, FROM THE SAME VIEWPOINT, IN 1990 (RIGHT)

Eaton Road (Watling Street)

The straightness of Eaton Road indicates its Roman origin. Its Medieval name was Watling Street: it took travellers from Chester via Wroxeter (Shrewsbury) to London. The excavation of St Mary's chancel revealed a Roman cemetery alongside the Roman road.

On Handbridge (the road), note the architecture of the Sexton's House of St Mary's Church (1887) and opposite, numbers 65 and 67 (Professor Newstead's houses—see chapter 6), built in 1899 by John Douglas. Ebury Street takes its name from the first Baron Ebury, Robert Grosvenor, third son of the first Marquess of Westminster.

On the right hand side of Eaton Road many of the Victorian houses are now guest houses, including the King's Guest House, which was formerly a dormitory of the King's School.

PHOTO—LEN MORGAN

▲ SEXTON'S HOUSE—ARCHITECT, JOHN DOUGLAS

PHOTO—LEN MORGAN

▲ KING'S GUEST HOUSE, 14 EATON ROAD IN 1985 (FORMERLY A DORMITORY FOR THE KING'S SCHOOL)

The four houses (36—42 Eaton Road), built by a Shropshire farmer before World War I, make up a single terrace and date from 1855. They were originally known as Wilton Terrace. In 1941 No 40, known as St Michael's, was bought by the Redfern family, who ran the well-known St Michael's Secretarial College there until 1971. The present owners, Anne and Bernard Beatty, have kept the original name, St Michael's, but would like to see the name Wilton Terrace, restored.

In the early 1930s a major housing development introduced Appleyards Lane, Eaton Avenue, Watling Crescent, Greenwood Avenue and Eccleston Avenue. The original housing layout was interspersed with small developments in the 1960s.

ST MICHAEL'S, NO 40 EATON ROAD, ▶ (FORMERLY PART OF WILTON TERRACE).

PHOTO—LEN MORGAN

Cremation Urn Found in Eaton Road

Wendy and Donald McIntyre came to live at 33, Eaton Road in 1968, one of a group of new houses built by Messrs Warringtons on what had formerly been allotments. In 1981, adding a porch to the front of their house, workmen found a 28 cm tall pot in the foundations, which the Grosvenor Museum identified as a Roman cinerary urn. It still contained the ashes and bone fragments of a cremated human. The orange-ware pot had been made at Holt cAD 100 (possibly off-loaded at Heronbridge and for sale outside the Garrison). This is one of several cremation burials found along Eaton Road.

Today the urn resides proudly on a shelf in their home, only a short distance from where it was buried nearly 2000 years ago.

WENDY WITH HER 1981 DISCOVERY ▲

PHOTO—LEN MORGAN

◀ THE OLDEST HOUSES IN HANDBRIDGE

NOS 15, 17, 19, 21, 23 AND 25 EATON ROAD WERE BUILT C1820* AND ARE PROBABLY THE OLDEST HOUSES IN HANDBRIDGE. THE TITHE MAP (1842) CLEARLY IDENTIFIES THE THREE PAIRS OF HOUSES (SEE THE INSIDE BACK COVER). THE 1862 ELECTORAL ROLL SHOWS THE APPLEYARD FAMILY LIVING AT NO 21.

* REVISED LIST OF BUILDINGS OF SPECIAL ARCHITECTURAL OR HISTORIC INTEREST

Belgrave Park Estate

In 1970 a partnership was formed between the Grosvenor Estate, Thomas Warrington and Sons Ltd (builders), Austin Vernon & Partners (architects) and Beresford Adams and Son (selling agents) to develop the Belgrave Park Estate. It was planned as a private estate of 140 luxury homes on land leased from the 6th Duke of Westminster.

The first house was occupied on 24th June, 1973 (by the co-author of this book) and the last on 4th December, 1987. All the houses are now freehold

▲ PICTURE FROM WARRINGTON'S BELGRAVE PARK CATALOGUE

and the estate has been adopted by the City Council. A feature of the estate is the street-naming—Audley and Clarendon, which originate from the Grosvenor family's London holdings and from their aristocratic associates Berkley, Chandos, Pembroke and Walton. The exception, Holbein, is named after the famous Court painter (Hans Holbein) (1497—1543) of Henry VII.

A 1737 map shows the ancient lane with the 'pen' at the entrance, built to secure stray animals and from which the farm and lane take their names. During World War II the Home Guard used this area for field training and rifle practice.

One of the tenants of Pinfold Farm was Thomas Appleyard (Jnr), who built Cheshire View, Appleyards Lane. To feed his 13 children, he rented 14 acres from the Grosvenors, including the farm, which had a large orchard (now part of Pinfold Court and Belgrave Park). He was the only son of Thomas Appleyard (Snr), head joiner to the 2nd Earl of Wilton of Heaton Hall near Manchester. The mother of Thomas Jnr, Elizabeth Swindley, was the daughter of the family that ran the smithy at Eccleston. Married into the family was John Douglas (Snr), whose son, John, was the famous local architect. John Douglas designed, and James Swindley made, the ornamental iron work of Chester's Eastgate Clock, installed in 1899 to commemorate Queen Victoria's Diamond Jubilee (1897).

PHOTO—THE HERITAGE CENTRE PHOTOSURVEY

▲ MR HENRY WITTER AT HIS PINFOLD LANE FARM C1925

Exciting Books Written in Netherfield, Eaton Road, Handbridge

Chester Courant headline, 16th May 1962

Mary Margaret Kaye (1908—2004), author of the best selling historical novel, The Far Pavilions, lived at Netherfield, Eaton Road, Handbridge during 1961—63, when her husband, Brigadier G J Hamilton CB, CBE, DSO (later Major General) was Chief of Staff, Western Command. The book was made into a film, which was televised in 1984, and starred Omar Sharif, John Gielgud, Rossano Brazzi and Ben Cross.

'Mollie' was born in Simla, the summer capital of British India. She came from a line of high-ranking officers and statesmen, who served the Raj for nearly 200 years. Combining the busy life as the wife of an Army officer serving all over the world, and the mother of two children, she wrote and illustrated numerous children's books, detective stories and historical novels. In Handbridge she published Trade Wind (about the slave trade): in 1983 she featured in Radio 4's Desert Island Discs and in 1990 on television in The Gloria Hunniford Show.

▲ THE INTERIOR OF GREENBANK IN 1942

PHOTO—67/711 NATIONAL BUILDING RECORD NBR 5/A1

Greenbank is a Regency house built in 1820 for Alderman John Swarbrick Rodgers, merchant and glover. He owned a prosperous skinning and tanning business near the Old Dee Bridge.

In 1907 Edward Peter Jones, who had moved to Chester in 1906 and founded the Mersey Iron Works at Ellesmere Port, bought the house. He became a County Councillor (1913-45), a Justice of the Peace (1919-50) and Sheriff (1931). He died in 1960, leaving his home to the City of Chester to be used 'for the service of youth'.

PHOTO—1937 PAGEANT PROGRAMME

▲ ALD E P JONES JP CC

In 1974 Cheshire Education Committee sold eleven acres at the rear of the house to fund the refurbishment of the house for the Chester College of Further Education (now the catering unit of the West Cheshire College). In this way the terms of the bequest were fulfilled.

PHOTO—BOB JONES

▲ PETER JONES AND HIS WIFE DRIVE OFF IN STYLE!

◄ PETER JONES OVERSEEING THE BUILDING WORK 1930s

▼ OPPOSITE GREENBANK WAS THE BEAUTIFUL EATON HALL LODGE (NOW DEMOLISHED). THE SITE IS STILL DISCERNIBLE AND THE FORMER EATON HALL DRIVE CAN BE TRACED THROUGH THE WOODS

PHOTO—JOHN TOMLINSON WHOSE GRANDFATHER IS EXTREME RIGHT

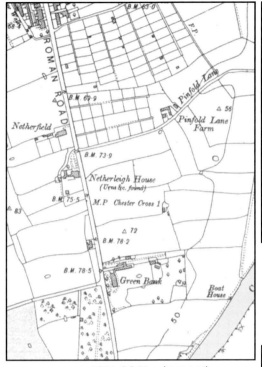

▲ 1911 OS MAP (EXTRACT)

THE MAP SHOWS ...

<u>NETHERFIELD HOUSE</u>: HOME OF THE ARMY BRIGADE COMMANDER, CHESTER DISTRICT.

<u>NETHERLEIGH HOUSE</u>: (SEE PP 3 & 4) DURING WORLD WAR II, A TEST PILOT, MAURICE HART, OWNED THE HOUSE, WHICH NOW BELONGS TO DR T D S HOLLIDAY, ONE TIME CHIEF PATHOLOGIST AT THE CHESTER HOSPITALS.

<u>ALLOTMENTS</u>: ABOVE PINFOLD LANE, WHICH BECAME THE SITE OF THE 1930S ESTATE (APPLEYARDS LANE, EATON AVENUE, WATLING CRESCENT, GREENWOOD AVENUE AND ECCLESTON AVENUE).

<u>GREEN FIELDS</u>: BELOW PINFOLD LANE WITH PINFOLD LANE FARM AND THE SITE OF BELGRAVE PARK ESTATE.

<u>GREENBANK</u>: (SEE OPPOSITE PAGE)

DURING WORLD WAR II, A STICK OF BOMBS WAS DROPPED IN THE AREA. ONE BOMB FELL AT THE ENTRANCE TO WHERE BELGRAVE PARK NOW STANDS. THE REPAIRED DAMAGE TO THE WALL OF NETHERLEIGH HOUSE CAN BE SEEN AS THE LIGHT COLOURED AREA. ▲

ANOTHER BOMB FELL JUST BEYOND HERONBRIDGE. THE CRATER IN THE FIELD STILL EXISTS. NOTE THE ROWING EIGHT PRACTISING ON THE RIVER DEE IN THE BACKGROUND. ▼

▼ PINFOLD LANE FARM IN 1975 WITH ECCLESTON AVENUE IN THE BACKGROUND

▼ HERONBRIDGE, THE HOME OF BRIAN WARRINGTON (DECEASED), FAMILY BUILDER OF LOCAL HOSPITALS, SCHOOLS, FACTORIES AND HOUSING. EARLIER THE ASSIZE JUDGES LODGED THERE.

COMPARE THE FARM OUTBUILDING ON THE RIGHT WITH THE PICTURE ON PAGE 159

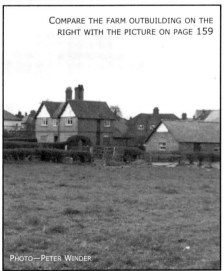

On the boundary of Handbridge lies Heronbridge (OE *HYRNE*=corner ie bend of the river + OE *BRYCG*=bridge or crossing), which was, prior to 1824, called Ironbridge. Here, in 1929, was discovered a Roman semi-industrial settlement straddling Eaton Road (*Watling Street*) to Eccleston, Aldford (*Old Ford*) and Whitchurch (*Mediolanum*). This settlement was occupied until at least AD 350.

Recent excavations (by Chester Archæological Society under Dr David Mason) have uncovered a number of graves. They had been plundered centuries earlier, the tombstones smashed, most of the bones thrown away and the valuables stolen. Fragments of a Roman tombstone were found inside a rock-cut grave, the largest piece of which (see photograph) is now on display in the Grosvenor Museum. It shows the head of a female figure reclining on a couch with a garland above her head, and the hand of a larger figure (which has otherwise disappeared) resting on her shoulder. The stone must have been the memorial to a man and his wife, or perhaps, to a man (or woman) and child. The tombstone is a standard Roman memorial called a 'funerary banquet', showing the dead person as a semi-divine figure feasting in the after life.

Also excavated was a quay, where small boats could tie up at high tide.

▲ ROMAN TOMBSTONE—SEE TEXT   ▲ TWO ROMAN ROCK-CUT GRAVES—SEE TEXT

HANDBRIDGE AREA HISTORY GROUP—VISIT TO THE ROMAN DIG AT HERONBRIDGE ▼

FROM LEFT TO RIGHT:
LEN MORGAN; JOAN MORGAN; PHIL MACEY; DR DAVID MASON; NOEL ST JOHN WILLIAMS; IAN BIRCHENOUGH; GERALD PUGH; A VISITOR